God's Blueprint

What does the Old Testament really say?

Steve Maltz

Saffron Planet
PO Box 2215
Ilford IG1 9TR
UK
T: +44 (0) 208 551 1719
E: contact@saffronplanet.net
W: www.sppublishing.com

ISBN 978-0-9562296-7-0

Cover design by Phil Maltz
Typeset by CRB Associates, Potterhanworth, Lincolnshire
Printed in the United Kingdom

Reviews

We've been "Maltzed" yet again! How does this guy do it? Everything Steve Maltz writes leaves me reeling. I am amazed at the consistently high level of his books. This latest offering ticks all the right boxes with me. Steve's goal is to be soundly biblical and very practical in his applications, yet he deals with matters that could so easily be dry as dust. Namely, what does the Old Testament really say? Yes, I know: you thought you knew, didn't you? Well I thought I knew and I've been a Bible teacher for fifty years! In reviewing this book I've learned a lot I simply didn't know before! I'm glad I know it now!

Our Lord Jesus the Messiah had a view of the Hebrew Scriptures (the Old Testament) that was stratospheric! He could not have given it higher value in His own daily life and in the training of the disciples. Jesus lived and breathed the Hebrew Scriptures: His Father's precious Word. If we are to follow Him and learn from Him, our determination needs to be as intense as His. That's why Steve's book is essential reading.

Here is an overview of the entire Old Testament library, emphasizing the Jewishness of it and the deep meanings to be unearthed from the Hebrew text. I found it to be fascinating and very faith building. If you think you can't afford it (!), sell your shirt to buy it! (**Chris Hill**, **Bible teacher, speaker and broadcaster**)

Steve Maltz is fast becoming the modern heir of C. S. Lewis – someone who can address his generation in a culturally attuned manner, and yet put across profound spiritual truths with an easy and engaging style. Averaging two books a year over the past five years, Maltz looks set to overtake some of the more established authors – if sheer output is a measure!

A blueprint is a standardized specification from which goods or processes can be precisely replicated. A blueprint in essence represents perfection. Deviations from the blueprint design represent a missing of the mark, less than perfection, and with possibly dangerously defective properties. Maltz explains how God has set out His blueprint for right relationship with Himself – through a Chosen People and through a Teaching (Torah). We all know that God's blueprint has been largely ignored down through history, by individuals and by a society made up of individuals. But more than this, the blueprint reveals the coming Son – the Saviour of mankind, and the One with whom we can all call upon in faith and repentance, as Saviour.

So what is this book? In essence it is a broad-brush painting of what we call "The Old Testament", the book that makes up three-quarters of our Bible and yet one with which many Christians frankly struggle. *God's Blueprint* is Maltz's attempt to help us see the broad connections, the beautiful bigger picture revealing both God's heart and God's righteous standards. Whilst the big picture is drawn with broad strokes, it is delivered by Maltz with sufficient fine detail drawn out in fine brush strokes to reveal huge truths that are often missed even by the diligent student. In other words this is not just another essay on the big events of the Old Testament, it shows God's connected plan to draw humans into right relationship with Himself, and through Himself, with each other.

There is one other big advantage to this useful short book. Maltz has an engaging style and a biblically astute understanding which he shares in an engaging manner. This book is a reasonably easy read, made more so by Maltz's reverent use of light humour and occasional irony.

What do readers achieve at the end of a reading of this new book? Certainly a better understanding of the interconnectedness of not only the Old Testament but the way it engages with the New. We have to remind ourselves from time to time that the Scriptures with which the Lord Jesus was familiar and which He fulfilled and which He expounded and proclaimed, was the Old Testament. If it was important to Jesus, then it has to be important to us as well! Maltz's book helps to put the whole Old Testament into a recognizable context. *God's Blueprint* is a "road map" to help us navigate the bigger obstacles to understanding.

The structure of *God's Blueprint* is straightforward. Divided into two parts, the first is a tour at rapid pace through all the Old Testament ("WORD"). This section consists of eleven chapters with chapter titles in the inimitable Maltz style, such as: Patriarchs and troubled hearts; Teachings and bleatings; Trouble and strife and; We told you so! The second part ("THEMES") consists of three chapters with Maltz's reflections on what the Old Testament Scriptures reveal about God, hence – Chapter 12: Some things we learn about God; Chapter 13: Some things we learn about man; and Chapter 14: Some other things we learn.

Overall, this is a useful addition to the serious student's library, and firmly at the top end of the popular theology genre, and modestly priced. It will also make a nice present for younger Christians, who need to get up to speed on the Scriptures, before moving onto heavier material.

Highly recommended – 5*

(Peter Sammons, author of *The Birth of Christ* and *One Flesh* – both published by Glory to Glory Publications)

God's Blueprint is a survey of the Hebrew Scriptures approached and written in the author's own inimitable style. Steve Maltz teaches and informs in a contemporary, entertaining and respectful way, while also teasing out the Hebraisms of Scripture. Steve leads the reader on a country walk taking in the off-the-beaten-track scenery, and breathing the air of God's people including the prophets, priests and kings from Genesis to Malachi. He explains how God grabs our attention and the unexpected choice of people He used to carry out His purposes – even using those who oppose Him to bring about His desired response and direction for His chosen people. Guiding them, even when they have deviated, drawing them back into travelling God's way and to His schedule. The Jews, he claims, have an undeniable future.

Using the Hebrew Scriptures the author walks on through the art gallery of time. Taking the Prophets and the Psalms he points to God's brush strokes that speak of Jesus, and how He is colourfully and unmistakably splashed all over the place – His birth, life, death, and reign on earth.

Explaining the Hebraic meaning of words and phrases as the author does on occasions, deepens and enlarges our understanding of God's Word to man. This is a book that should be found on every Christian's bookshelf. It is a book that will be constantly dipped into as a refreshing Bible study aid.

(Malcolm Baker, Pointers ministries)

With thanks . . .

. . . to the usual team for helping me to put this book together. You know who you are and therein lies your reward ;-)

Contents

Prologue

The journey begins and I am so excited at what God will show us through His Word.

First, some ground-rules. This is not an exhaustive commentary on the Hebrew Scriptures, but rather a meandering and we won't be visiting the popular beauty spots featured in the glossy travel brochures. Instead, we will be lifting up stones and poking around in the undergrowth. We will also look upwards and outwards at the bigger picture and, following the unique quirks of the Hebrew mind, we will be making connections, sometimes in unusual places, often crossing over boundaries erected by theologians to keep us nice and ordered. Not so much the highways, as the byways; not so much the purple prose as the small print.

As I have stressed many times in recent books, there are two *mindsets* that dominate the thinking of modern man, Christians included. These are the *Greek* mindset, perhaps best expressed in the phrase, "Know thyself!" and the *Hebraic* mindset, which focuses on *knowing God*. Now here's the problem in a nutshell. The Bible was written using the Hebraic mindset, but, these days tends to be understood using the Greek mindset. This means that we tend to see the Bible predominantly as a source for *our* thoughts and actions. There is nothing wrong with that, but what is often neglected is *God Himself*.

There's no better way of getting to know the One we are going to spend eternity with, than by reading *His* Book. There's so much we can learn about Him from the Hebrew Scriptures, from the developing story of His dealings with His people. I would go as far as to say that these Scriptures, the Old Testament, are there to provide us with a *blueprint*, a design plan, of God's heart. *God's blueprint.*

So that has been my aim with this book. In the first part there is a complete sweep of the Hebrew Scriptures, from Genesis to Malachi. I have gone, as far as I can, for broad chronological accuracy rather than neat divisions. So Job comes between Genesis and Exodus and the two books of Chronicles straddle the Psalms. Also, where possible I have placed the prophets as close as I could to the narrative they refer to, so we can have historical context. It may all seem a bit of a mess, but I think that the Scriptures will speak to you in new ways.

In the second part, I strip out all of the themes uncovered so far and displayed logically (how Greek is that!), so that we can start to see some important principles on how God deals with His people. There may be some surprises here for you, there certainly were for me! Then, in the Epilogue, key observations are made about God and about man.

I am particularly excited because in this book I'll be using a brand-new translation, the *One New Man Bible*[1]. It will be like walking a well-worn route, but with better-fitting boots. I am prepared for a dash of unfamiliarity in the wording, but I am buoyed up by the knowledge that the words I will read are perhaps the closest to the original intention of the writers (and Writer!) that I've ever experienced. I won't qualify that statement, instead we will just let the journey itself provide its own commentary.

It is time for us to pore over the blueprint . . .

Note

1. The One New Man Bible is published by TP Press (www.tppress.org) in the USA and distributed in the UK by Saffron Planet Publishing, www.sppublishing.com. There is more information about this Bible translation in the advert at the end of this book. As a Bible with a tighter than average link with the Jewish Masoretic text, there will be instances where the numbering of verses will differ from other translations. These places will be indicated when relevant.

PART ONE
Word

**A meander through the Hebrew Scriptures
with some observations, remarks
and curiosities**

Patriarchs and troubled hearts

The Book of Genesis

No, I'm not going to start at the usual place, the Creation story. Whole volumes of books have been written on this; in fact I own a book that is basically a commentary on just the first seven words of Genesis. All I will say is that the universe, the world and all that lies within were not just spoken into existence, but **shouted** into being and that God's first command to mankind was hardly whispered.

> *And God blessed them and God said to them, "Be fruitful! Multiply! Fill the earth! Subdue it and have dominion over the fish of the sea and over the fowl of the air and over every living thing that moves upon the earth!"*
> (Genesis 1:28)

You can sense the immediacy and the urgency here and we are going to discover that the Bible is a lot more action-oriented than we could ever imagine. God does a lot of empathizing (shouting) and the Hebrew language lends itself well to this. This should be no surprise, as it is God's chosen language for expressing His ideas in the most direct manner. The trouble is, of course, that mostly we're not native Hebrew scholars and have to make do with English translations, produced by flawed human beings.

This is not so say that Bible translators are any more flawed than the rest of us, but we have to accept that every translation we read is always going to be tinged by *other* factors, including the motives, background and mindset of the individuals or committees tasked with this function. The reason why the *One New Man Bible* excites me is that the *flawed human being* who translated/edited it, has declared that his primary motivation is to convey the Hebraic context as best as he can, even if the end result is not necessarily tidy or poetic or politically (and religiously) correct! This will do for me and, hopefully, for you too.

  Here's an interesting take on the Cain and Abel story. The usual understanding of God's preference for Abel's sacrifice is that his was a sacrifice that involved the shedding of blood, whereas Cain's was of the fruits of his labour, literally the fruits of the ground. *And we all know that God prefers the former, don't we?* Yes we do, but it doesn't necessarily mean that this can be the *only* interpretation. After all, someone had to be the "tiller of the ground". There may be more than one lesson, here, if we are prepared to accept that, with Scripture, *not everything is black or white*. Our tidy minds would prefer if it was, because that's how we have been trained to think, as a result of the *Greek mindset* that is the bedrock of our thought processes in the Western world. Not so with the things of God, I'm afraid.

  Let's read the opening salvo of this murder scenario.

> *"And in process of time it came to pass that Cain brought an offering to the LORD from the fruit of the ground."*
> (Genesis 4:3)

Perhaps the real issue here was one of timeliness, that Cain didn't bring his offering at the right time. Perhaps the intention was good, but that there was a diary malfunction? How often have you and I made sacrifices to God of our time and resources, only to be met with silence or correction because we haven't waited for God's leadings and timings?

Yet we can't excuse Cain's reaction to his rejection, which indicated that there was a real problem with his heart:

> "And the LORD said to Cain, "Why are you so angry? And why has your countenance fallen? Behold, if you do well, you will be accepted. And if you do not do well, sin sits waiting at the door, and its desire is to possess you, but you can rule over it."
> (Genesis 4:6–7)

Unfortunately, this good advice was not heeded.

Surely we can see that Scripture, as energised by the Holy Spirit, can say different things to different people, or even say different things to the *same* people. This story speaks to me of both *timeliness* and *the quality of our sacrifice*, as Scripture implies both and also of Cain's catastrophic reaction. What we *mustn't* do, of course, is read into Scripture things that are *not* there in the text, or that are the promptings of our wildest imaginings.

After Cain has done the evil deed, God exclaims: "*What have you done? The voice of your brother's blood cries to Me from the ground*" (Genesis 4:10). This is the first mention of *blood* in Scripture. But is there more here than meets the eye?

The Hebrew word here for "blood" is *dam*. Also, the word for "ground" (in the same verse) is *adamah*. We notice that these two words are very similar to the word for "man", *adam*. In English this wouldn't necessarily be an issue, but with Hebrew it is *always* an issue, because of the way the language is constructed, with a great emphasis on root words. What we have here are three words – man, ground and blood – all sharing the same root and all connected (with man being formed from the dust of the ground). Blood is what sustains man and we are aware of the verse in Leviticus:

> "For the life of the flesh is in the blood."
> (Leviticus 17:11)

We will keep a watchful eye on this theme as we progress. But first, we skip a couple of Chapters to Noah and his ark.

First cast your minds back to your Sunday school days (those of you who went), to the usual depiction of Noah's ark. A search of Google would re-inforce the romantic image of a wooden boat-shaped craft, with animals peering out of every orifice. That's not what Scripture says.

"Make a box of gopher wood for yourself. You will make compartments in the box, and will cover it within and without with atonement." (Genesis 6:14)

The word that is usually translates as "ark" is *tebah*, which literally means chest or box. It is the same word used for the basket of bulrushes that transported the infant Moses down the river. Now, think about it, Noah's *box* doesn't have a very romantic ring about it. It doesn't seem special enough, it is too *mundane* a word. This is, interestingly, a key point and a theme worth developing. It's the issue of the *holy and the mundane*. Do we separate the "things of God" from the "things of man"? Are some objects innately holy? This may not be a major issue in the case of *Noah's box*, but perhaps there are better examples later on . . .

You may have noticed another anomaly in the verse just quoted. Why has the last word, normally translated as "pitch" appear here as *atonement*? Well, we have to realize that here, as in all cases, the translators have to look at the single Hebrew word and decide, from the context of the passage, what its meaning is. This can be a complex process as, with biblical Hebrew, no vowels are used. So what we have here is a word of three consonants, KFR, with the following possible meanings; *ransom/atonement, bribe, asphalt, pitch, henna, village*. Although the usual translation of this word elsewhere in the Hebrew Scriptures is *atonement*, this is the only place where it is usually translated as *pitch*, in the sense of the mucky gooey stuff that is used for waterproofing.

Of course it makes good sense contextually to translate it as *pitch*, in the sense of waterproofing the outside of the ark/box, but perhaps not the inside. Also *henna* would make sense as a deodorant against the pong of the animals inside the ark/box. But what of *atonement*? Is there a spiritual context here, concerning the salvation of those within the ark?

Our Greek way of thinking could only accept *one* of these explanations, but think of the multi-layered picture here of God's concern for their safety (waterproofing on the outside), comfort (air freshener) and spiritual wellbeing. It may be a different, even extraordinary, way of interpreting God's Word, but who said that the Bible was an ordinary book?

When the waters had receded and Noah's family left the ark/box, we get the curious episode of the drunken patriarch in the tent. Let's face it, if Noah was going to plant a vineyard, you would expect him to sample his produce, with the odd lapse of judgement due to over-sampling! So here he was, drunk and uncovered, something that should never be witnessed by close relatives, according to the prohibitions in Leviticus. But Ham, his middle son, witnessed it, something avoided by the other two sons. We then get the curious Scripture:

> *"And Noah awoke from his wine and knew what his younger son had done to him. And he said, "Cursed be Canaan; a servant of servants will he be to his brothers." And he said, "Blessed be the LORD God of Shem; and Canaan will be his servant".*
> (Genesis 9:24–26)

The really curious thing about this is that Ham was *not* the younger son. But Canaan *was* Ham's youngest son and, as he was the one to be cursed, there can be scope for *reading between the lines* to suggest an unspeakable act committed by this youngest grandson. It is perhaps valid to do so when we read of the subsequent history of the descendants of Canaan and what they got up to and also when we consider the extreme nature of the curse, that the Canaanite people *were never to flourish*. Bear this in mind later on in our explorations.

The next time we hear God really shouting was when He turned his attention to a man called Abram, living in Ur and exclaimed, *"Get yourself out of here!"* (Genesis 12:1). Abram, this mighty man of faith, heeded the call and earned the biggest entry in the *Great Hall of Faith* (Hebrews 11). Yet he had his lapses, before we distance him through bleary-eyed eulogy. He was *one of us*, as are all of the heroes of the Hebrew Scriptures. The man who had met with God and had been promised an incredible legacy had a faith-lapse when he urged his wife, Sarai, to pretend to be his sister, as otherwise the Pharaoh might kill him. These lies ironically brought plagues on Pharaoh, who had unwittingly activated a vital clause in Abram's first draft contract with God.

> *"And I shall bless those who bless you and curse the one who curses you . . ."*
> (Genesis 12:3)

Blessings and curses. This is a theme that is going to recur again and again as we continue our journey into God's Word.

Abram's contract was restated to him in a vision of such intensity that God had to remind him not to be fearful.

> *After these things the word of the LORD came to Abram in a vision, saying,* **"Do not be in awe***, Abram! I* AM *your Shield! Your reward will be exceedingly great."*
> (Genesis 15:1)

The expression in bold, **Do not be in awe**, is a uniquely powerful command and has no exact English translation. It is rendered even stronger here with the use of God's personal title, I AM (*anoki* in Hebrew), a *royal* designation of the highest degree. We must look out for these things in the Hebrew

Scriptures, because what is most important for God, such as the proclamation of a covenant with Abram, ought to be the most important for us too.

Later on Abram gets a name change to *Abraham* and we join him next when he has his meeting with the three men, one of whom is the Lord Himself, arguably in the person of a pre-incarnate Jesus (for more on this I urge you to read my book, *Jesus, Man of Many Names*).

The three men were discussing Abraham as they looked down at the twin horrors, Sodom and Gomorrah.

> *"For I know him, that he will command his children and his household after him and they will keep the Way of the LORD, to do acts of loving kindness and judgment, so the LORD may bring upon Abraham that which He has spoken of him."*
> (Genesis 18:19)

Other translations use the lower-case *the way*, diminishing its significance, but the *One New Man Bible* has it in upper-case, as *the Way*, reminiscent of the designation of the early Church in the Book of Acts (e.g. Acts 9:2).

Which is it to be? The word itself, *derech*, offers no clues, but the context perhaps speaks, because here we see defined what "the Way of the Lord" is; *to do acts of loving kindness and judgement*. There are over 50 other uses of this term in the Hebrew Scriptures, so we will keep a watchful eye on this one.

Returning to this story, God is about to destroy Sodom and Gomorrah, but was willing to listen to Abraham's pleadings that if just 50 righteous can be found, then 45, then 40, then 30, then 20, then 10 . . . Although this was ultimately in vain, it does demonstrate what seems to be a general principle with God. *He is willing to work with small numbers!* Remember that one for later on.

Before we leave this story there's a sordid episode that may pique our interest. The story of Lot's daughters (Genesis

19:30–38), who got their father drunk and did unspeakable things to him. The results of this were the peoples of Moab and Ammon, who, just like the Canaanites, were not exactly going to flourish in later days. Again we may be seeing a general principle being played out here.

In fact we see this in action when Abraham gives instructions on his choice of wife for his son, Isaac to his servant:

> *"And I shall make you swear by the LORD, the God of heaven and the God of the earth, that you will not take a wife for my son of the daughters of the Canaanites among whom I dwell"*
> (Genesis 24:3)

Interbreeding with the cursed Canaanites was out of the question. Also this applied to the chosen son of the next generation, Jacob.

> *"And Isaac called Jacob and blessed him and charged him and said to him, "You will not take a wife of the daughters of Canaan . . ."*
> (Genesis 28:1–2)

But not so for the *un-chosen* elder brother, Esau.

> *"Now these are the descendants of Esau, who is Edom. Esau took for his wives from the daughters of Canaan."*
> (Genesis 36:1–2)

The chosen line is being kept as pure as possible. We will follow this line as our story develops.

The next generation is dominated by the adventures of Joseph, Jacob's last-but-one son, he of the *supposed* coat of many colours (in the original Hebrew text it was actually a poncho, or long tunic, of unspecified colouring). We read of Joseph's dream, of his dominion over his brothers and his less-than-wise decision to boast about it to them. Yet this lapse of judgement set off a chain of events, a bumpy ride for all concerned, leading to reconciliation (between the brothers) and fulfilled prophecy (Genesis 15:13), as well as the fulfilment of the dream itself! Good can certainly come out of bad, if you wait long enough.

Here's an interesting aside, that should seek to show how Bible translations can be affected by the times in which we live. Let's turn to Genesis 38:2:

> *And Judah saw there a daughter of a certain Canaanite, whose name was Shua, and he took her and went in to her.*

Quite a graphic description of what Judah did. Eh? This is also how the King James Version described the act. Now let's examine some more modern "gentler" versions. *He married her and slept with her* (CEB), *he married her and lay with her* (NIV), *he married her* (GNB, NLT), *he married her, they went to bed* (The Message). Quaint, isn't it? But it does serve to show us how Bible text can be meddled with to fit in with our perceived needs. Now I wonder how the URV (Urban Rap Version) would translate that verse!?

Before we leave this action-packed first book of the Bible, here is an interesting observation on the life of Joseph. Firstly, returning to what I had earlier called the vital clause in Abram's first draft contract with God:

> *"And I shall bless those who bless you and curse the one who curses you . . ."*
> (Genesis 12:3)

Joseph was a blessing to those who treated him well, whether it was Potiphar (who made him the overseer of his house), the keeper of the prison (who made him an unofficial pastor of the prisoners) and the Pharaoh himself (who gave him the highest authority over the land).

Finally, it is interesting to notice that the two key injustices against Joseph in his life, both involved his tunic – "proof" of his demise to Jacob (Genesis 37:32) and "proof" of his dalliance with his master's wife (Genesis 39:12). There has to be a spiritual significance there, but that's one for you to determine, dear reader.

The Book of Job

What's this mixed-up fellow doing in a place like this? Yes, you expected to see the Book of Exodus, as the second book in the Torah, but my intention is to be, as far as I can, *chronologically* accurate rather than "traditionally" accurate. Despite there being much discussion on the subject, the majority view is that Job lived approximately at the same time as the patriarchs Abraham, Isaac and the others. So, before we get the adventures of Moses, we make a slight detour eastwards to the Land of Uz, where *there was a man called Job and that man was honest, unsophisticated and upright and one that revered God and turned aside from evil* (Job 1:1).

This is an important book and is the first in history to take seriously the question of why bad things happen to good people. It does so through a series of conversations between Job – afflicted in many ways as a result of a "deal" between God and Satan – and his three friends. Read those yourself to follow the thread of the arguments, as my intention is to concentrate on God's perspective, as He reacts to these arguments and *tells them where it's really at!* Because, by doing so, we'll get a good perspective on the real relationship between the Creator and the created in the grand scheme of things.

So how did Job cope with this dramatic reversal of his fortunes? He starts off by cursing the day he was born. Wouldn't we do the same, after all there's only so much physical, spiritual and emotional pain one person can take! His greatest fear had been realised:

"For the thing which I greatly feared has come upon me, and that of

which I was afraid of has come to me. I was not in safety, neither did I
have rest, nor was I quiet, yet trouble came."
(Job 3:25–26)

It is probably the greatest fear that any of us could have, the
fear that our lives can suddenly and unexpectedly be blighted
by misfortune, be it disease or bereavement or anything else of
that ilk. Job had copped the lot! Yet his faith in God was unswerv-
ing. He never denied His Maker, but he still needed answers. *Is*
it something I have done? If so, what can I do about it? Why are you
not listening to me?

*"I shall say to God, **Do not condemn me!** Show me why You contend*
with me".
(Job 10:2)

This is followed by a gradual descent into despair, although his faith held strong. He makes one final plea for his
defence:

"Oh that one would listen to me! Behold, here is my plea, let the Almighty
answer me and the indictment which my adversary has written! Surely
I would take it upon my shoulder, binding it to me as a crown. I would
declare to him the number of my steps, as a prince I would go near to
him. If my land cries against me, or that the furrows weep together; if I
have eaten the strength of it without money, or have caused its owners
to breathe out their life, let thistles grow instead of wheat and cockle
instead of barley."
(Job 31:35–40)

Then God, the Heavenly judge, issues His verdict.

"Then the Lord *answered Job out of the whirlwind and said, Who is*
this that darkens counsel by words without knowledge?"
(Job 38:1–2)

This sentence provides, in many ways, the crux of mankind's problem. *Words without Knowledge*. How often have our theologians, philosophers, historians and scientists, when trying to fathom out the Mind of God, have done so from their own limited perspectives, theories, suppositions and clevernesses? Unless God has truly enlightened them, then they speak, as did Job and his associates, *words without knowledge*.

God then lays out His credentials, *as if He really needed to defend Himself!*

Where was man when I created the world, eh?
Who arranged the land, sea and stars correctly, so that each could fulfil its purpose, eh?
How did time and the seasons come into being, without which humanity could never flourish, eh?
Who decided the span and purpose for each individual human life on this earth, eh?
Who set the patterns and characteristics of all life, from the deer to the donkeys to the wild ox and the ostrich, eh?

Then God lays down a challenge:

"Moreover the LORD answered Job, and said, Will the one who contends with the Almighty instruct Him? The one who reproves God, let him answer it."
(Job 40:1–2)

You could imagine the silence, then the nervous gulps, then Job's admission:

"Behold, I am vile. What will I answer You? I shall lay my hand upon my mouth. I have spoken once, but I shall not answer. Yea, twice, but I shall proceed no further."
(Job 40:4–5)

God continues in the same vein, eager to drive a very important point home, by switching attention from Himself to man.

Who's the righteous One here?
Can you perform My mighty acts?
Can you bring down the proud and the wicked?
Could you create and sustain such a creature as a
hippopotamus?
Can you tame a leviathan?

Job is firmly put in his place, having dared to question God's motives behind His actions:

"Then Job answered the LORD, and said, I know that You can do everything, and that no thought can be withheld from You. Who is the one who hides counsel without knowledge? Truly I have uttered what I do not understand, things too wonderful for me, which I did not know. Hear, I beseech You, and I shall speak: I shall demand of You, and You declare to me. I have heard of You by the listening of the ear, but now my eye sees You. Therefore I abhor myself, and repent in dust and ashes."
(Job 42:1–6)

Job, despite being a man bereft and battered, is now brought to repentance. God rebuked Job's companions for talking nonsense and urges them to take a burnt offering to Job, who alone will plead their case, taking the role as priest before the Lord.

Then Job's ordeal was over, *the LORD also accepted Job* (Job 42:9) and he was rewarded with twice as much as he had lost.

"After this Job lived a hundred forty years and saw his sons and his sons' sons, four generations."
(Job 42:16)

The story of Job should be a lesson for us all. Whatever life throws at us, we are urged to mirror the initial reaction of Job

(*The* LORD *gave and the* LORD *has taken away. Blessed be the name of the* LORD), rather than the advice from his wife (*Curse God and die*). We can't possibly know God's intentions at any time for us, though we know that, *if we are in covenant with Him*, then all He does for us is ultimately for our own good. He could choose to take us out of this world prematurely, or allow us to suffer physically or emotionally for extended periods. There is no magic formula that can determine how God ought to be directing our lives at any given moment in time. True wisdom in these matters is only going to be available to us, one would imagine, when our mortal coil has been shaken off and we are sitting with God poring over the Book of our Life. Only then will it all make perfect sense. Until then . . .

We can't always expect to fully understand the Mind of God, but just to hold on to this truth:

> "*He is the Rock, His work is perfect, for all His ways are justice. A God of truth and without injustice, just and right is He.*"
> (Deuteronomy 32:4)

The Book of Exodus

The very name of this book (in Hebrew), *sh'mot* (=*names*), indicates that God is now starting to get really personal. It refers to the opening verse, *now these are the* **names** *of the children of Israel*. From the 70-strong family, all descendants of Abraham having entered Egypt, we now read of a ragged and unruly nation of 2 million plus *children of Israel*, who were to leave Egypt. But we're getting ahead of ourselves . . .

We read how the first salvation of God's people was through an ark, literally a *box* (tevah), covered with pitch. The story now repeats, with *Moses*, God's chosen leader of this new generation, also saved through a *box* (tevah) covered with pitch. Patterns appear a lot in the Hebrew Scriptures, we just need a nudge to find them, though a good knowledge of Hebrew also helps!

Here's another pattern. We zip forwards forty years and find Moses in exile from Egypt in the land of Midian.

". . . He sat down by a well."
(Exodus 2:15)

It was here that he found his wife, Zipporah. So what? It was also by a well that both Isaac (actually his servant) and Jacob met their wives. Is this co-incidence, intent (wells were the equivalent of today's laundrettes in terms of romantic encounters) or pattern?

Patterns seem to be a persistent feature of the Hebraic mind. I think God loves it when we make connections, it encourages us to roam with our thoughts, frees us from the fetters of structure and makes life reassuringly interesting and unpredictable. Some of you may, of course, disagree. Structure and predictability is the norm in our Greek culture. Everything in its place, nice and comfortable. But perhaps God sometimes wants us to peer over the fence at *unexpected possibilities*.

Jacob Prasch, the Bible teacher, noticed that the well where Jacob met Rachel was the same well where, over two thousand years later, Jesus met the Samaritan woman (John 4:6). He saw a pattern, a deeper one suggested by these stories. He saw Jacob having to wait for his beloved Rachel, with a marriage to her sister Leah first. He also saw Jesus coming for his beloved Jewish people, but not fully consummating this love until he first takes the Gentile Church and loves them too. The art of discovering and thinking about patterns is a rabbinic way of viewing scripture called *Midrash*. The full story of the *Women at the Well* can be seen on Jacob Prasch's ministry website at www.moriel. org/PDF/Newsletter/1997/3Q-1997b_The_Woman_at_the_ Well.pdf

Then there's a more obvious pattern. This is a time duration. It was the number of years that Moses spent waiting in Midian and his people spent fruitlessly wandering around in the desert.

It was also the number of days that Moses spent receiving the *Torah* on Sinai and, folding back the years, the days spent by Noah in his box, waiting for the rains to finish. It is, of course, the number *forty*. When you see this number in the Bible you can expect it to be attached to a period initiated by God, usually a time of testing or trial. It's a link in an invisible chain that traverses the whole Bible, including the New Testament (Jesus' time in the wilderness and his period of appearances after his death), connecting significant times when God was *really* working in someone's life.

Moses meets with God, as you know, at the burning bush. It is after this episode when He gives His full complete title to Moses.

> *"Moreover He said, "I AM the God of your father, the God of Abraham, the God of Isaac, and the God of Jacob . . ."*
> (Exodus 3:6)

You'll remember that the words "I AM" (*anoki* in Hebrew), are His personal title, a *royal* designation of the highest degree. He doesn't use these words lightly, so neither should we.

What He *isn't* saying is, *"I am the God of your father, the God of Abraham"*, in the sense of, *"Hey, I'm the God of . . ."*

What He *is* saying is, *"I AM the God of your father, the God of Abraham"*.

You see the difference? The NIV translates Exodus 4:12 thus:

> *"Now go; I will help you speak and will teach you what to say."*

This totally misses the power of the original intention, in the original Hebrew. Here's the ONM translation:

> *"Now go! I AM! I will be with your mouth and I will teach you what you will say."*

Yes, it doesn't read well in English, but it's what the Hebrew actually says. It pours God into His words, giving them extra strength and power as it shows us a God who is totally identifying Himself with His actions.

This pattern repeats all over Scripture and most translations, in their desire for a clean reading style, leave out this strong identifier, resulting in a tragic loss to their reader of the power in God's Word.

Here is a very purposeful passage that is full of God's intent:

> *"And you will say to him, 'The* Lord *God of the Hebrews has sent me to you saying,* **Send My people away!** *So they can serve Me in the wilderness. And behold, till now you would not listen. Thus says the* Lord*, By this you will know that I* am *the* Lord*! . . ."*
> (Exodus 7:16–17)

There can be no doubt Who is speaking and what He wants! Yet Pharaoh chose to ignore this. He hardened his heart, then had it hardened for him. Why would God do that? Well, the following passage reveals what is being played out here.

> *"And the* Lord *said to Moses,* **"Come** *in to Pharaoh! For I have strengthened his heart and the heart of his servants, so I could show these signs of Mine before him, and so you could tell in the ears of your son, and of your son's son, what things I have done in Egypt and My signs which I have done among them, so you will know how that I* am *the* Lord*."*
> (Exodus 10:1–2)

The telling word is the Hebrew word **bo** (come), usually mistranslated as "go". It sets the scene of stubborn old Pharaoh, sitting on his throne, his heart (and that of his servants) *hardened* (strengthened). Next to him stands God Himself, beckoning Moses to *come and join them* and take part in a drama that is going to impact history so strongly that people will be speaking of what is to come for generation after generation.

And why was Pharaoh's heart hardened? *So that future gener-ations should know that "I ᴀᴍ the Lᴏʀᴅ".* God was in charge. He still is, He is the Great Conductor (these scenes formed the backdrop centuries later to the events of Jesus' Last Supper, as he celebrated Passover with his disciples). It may seem unfair to us, when we witness how many Egyptian lives are going to be destroyed, but *only God knows the Big Picture.*

Moving on, Moses leads them out of Egypt and what is virtually the first interaction between God and His new nation.

"And it will be when the Lᴏʀᴅ brings you into the land of the Canaanites, as He swore to you and to your fathers and will give it to you, that you will set apart to the Lᴏʀᴅ all that opens the womb, and every firstling that comes of an animal which you have; the males will be the Lᴏʀᴅ's. And every firstling of a donkey you will redeem with a lamb, and if you will not redeem it, then you will break its neck, and you will redeem all the firstborn of man among your children."
(Exodus 13:11–13)

The firstborn of the Egyptians may have suffered the penalty for the sins of the Pharaoh, but the firstborns of the Hebrews are going to be set apart for the Lord. Does this make them important? It used to be in our culture, when the firstborn son inherited the estate and the secondborn was carted off to the Church to become unwilling clergy (that goes a long way to explain what went wrong in the Church at that time!) But in God's economy, we find that firstborns figure little in the key genealogies. For instance, here's the beginning of the line from Abraham; Isaac (second born), Jacob (second born), Judah (fourth born) . . .

Yet the firstborns are redeemed, set apart for God, a ritual, *pidyon haben*, that still exists in Judaism. In time, He chooses a tribe, the descendants of Levi, to take the place of the first-borns, whose role was to serve Him first in the tabernacle and later in the Temple. And what about now? We now gain our

redemption, not by matter of natural birth but by *new birth*.
Seems a lot fairer to me.

But the children of Israel are not safe yet. They've reached
the edge of the sea and are flapping about. They see the
chariots of the Egyptians behind them and the sea ahead of
them and their faith deserts them. *What kind of a mess have you
got us into, Moses? Let's go home now with the Egyptians.* Despite
this, God really hadn't finished with them and Moses boldly
proclaims,

> **"Do not be in awe!** *Stand still! See the salvation of the* LORD, *which He
> will show you today, for the Egyptians whom you have seen today,
> you will see them again no more forever. The* LORD *will fight for you,
> and you will hold your peace."*
> (Exodus 14:13–14)

That first command, that we saw earlier when Abram had
a vision of God, is a signal that something truly awesome is
going to happen and they are going to learn now (and swiftly
forget!) that *when the Lord fights for you*, you should expect
results! So the waters part, the Hebrews are saved and the
Pharaoh's army drowns. *The Lord fights for you.* Remember
that, it's an important principle, it's really the only thing that
keeps the Children of Israel alive in those turbulent times,
despite any thoughts they may have about their own strength
and power. Moses' victory song acknowledges this and sends
out a strong message to the nations that they are about to
encounter. *If you mess with us, you mess with the Lord, and you
really don't want to do that!*

> *"Then the chiefs of Edom will be amazed. Trembling will take hold of
> the mighty men of Moab. All the inhabitants of Canaan will melt away.
> Fear and terror will fall on them. By the greatness of Your arm they will
> be as still as a stone . . ."*
> (Exodus 15:15–16)

So much of God's character and how He deals with His people is demonstrated in these passages in Exodus. These are timeless truths and it is sad that so many in the Church neglect the Hebrew Scriptures, not wishing to involve themselves in the "back story" but would rather just bask in the Good News of Jesus Christ. Don't they wish to fully understand their Creator?

Here's one thing that we *consumer* Christians would do well to heed. God supplied all of the physical needs of the Children of Israel in the desert, but *no more* than they needed. Storing up *manna* for later was not an option!

> *"And Moses said, "Let no man leave any till morning." Nevertheless they did not listen to Moses, but some of them left of it until the morning and it bred worms and stank, and Moses was very angry with them."*
> (Exodus 16:19–20)

Just enough manna and when they needed it. How many of us have enough faith to trust that God will not abandon us, even if some of His interventions are at the eleventh hour, and sometimes at the *fifty-ninth minute* of the eleventh hour? Tell me about it!

But still they moaned (as do we when God refuses to stick to our timetables) and blamed Moses for their discomforts. But Moses put them right and reminded them what he had told them after they had crossed the Sea:

> *"Therefore the people contended with Moses and said, "Give us water so we can drink." And Moses said to them, "Why argue with me? Why do you tempt the LORD?"*
> (Exodus 17:2)

Moses was fed up with all of this *kvetching*. He was also weary and not a young man and needed to take advice from his father-in-law, Jethro, that perhaps it was time to delegate and *spread the load*. This was done to free him up for his primary mission:

"And you will teach them ordinances and Torah (Teaching) and will show them the Way in which they must walk and the work that they must do."
(Exodus 18:20)

We are back to *the Way*. Earlier we read that this was the mission of Abraham, *to do acts of loving kindness and judgment* and now we see this being re-inforced in the ministry of Moses in *how they must walk and the work they must do*. The Way hasn't changed and it is a central thread of all Scripture, second only to the awesome story of salvation. *The Way* is all about our actions, our deeds, our works. The Hebrew Scriptures are very much a practical manual for living.

And how do we know what to base our deeds and actions on? Well, the ten commandments, or, rather, *the ten statements*, are a good start. The full list is in Exodus 20. It is telling to see that, right at the beginning, God is being most personal.

"I AM the LORD your God Who has brought you out of the land of Egypt, out of the house of bondage."
(Exodus 20:2)

It couldn't be clearer Who is speaking. His personal title, followed by His unspeakable Name (depicted as LORD), then He reminds us of His relationship with us and clinches it with a further reminder of what He has done for His people.

He has our undivided attention.

Then He tells us the basic rules of life. To emphasise the really key one, He again adds His personal signature.

"You will not bow down yourself to them (other gods), or serve them, for I AM the LORD your God, a jealous God . . ."
(Exodus 20:5)

Unfortunately the breaking of this commandment was eventually to be their downfall. If only they had taken God more seriously. Perhaps we, too, don't take Him seriously enough. Who do we bow down to? Who do we serve? If God was a jealous God at the time of Moses, be convinced that He *still is now.*

And no episode demonstrates this more than what happened while the boss was away for forty days receiving these laws from God on Mount Sinai.

> *"And when the people saw that Moses delayed coming down from the mountain, the people gathered themselves together to Aaron and said to him, "Get up! Make gods for us that will go before us, for this Moses, the man who brought us up out of the land of Egypt, we do not know what has happened to him." And Aaron said to them, "Take off the golden earrings, which are in the ears of your wives, of your sons, and of your daughters and bring them to me." And all the people took off the golden earrings, which were in their ears and brought them to Aaron. And he took them from their hand and fashioned it in a mold, and he made a molten calf and they said, "This is your god, O Israel, that brought you up out of the land of Egypt."*
>
> (Exodus 32:1–4)

The golden calf. What *were* they thinking of? Did they forget what Moses had done for them? Could they not see where he had gone? What about the fire and the smoke and the quaking? Couldn't they see that Moses was *really doing business*? (I'm using a colloquialism here, not being disrespectful)

And as for Aaron! The man who has already acted as God's mouthpiece and priest and had seen so many miracles first hand, was re-fashioning golden earrings into an idol and calling it Israel's God? Had he gone mad? He even created an altar for this abomination and assigned a day of indulgence and debauchery to mark the occasion. Talk about digging himself into a bigger and bigger hole.

When Moses came down and exploded in righteous anger and forced the idolaters to eat the ground-up idol, before killing them, what was Aaron's excuse? After blaming the others, he came out with this classic line:

"And I said to them, 'Whoever has any gold, let them take it off.' So they gave it to me. Then I threw it into the fire and this calf came out."
(Exodus 32:24)

How Aaron retained his job after this fracas is a mystery to me, but just a reflection of the grace and unknowable plans of God, I suppose.

A telling phrase was when God had first alerted Moses to this outrage:

"They have turned aside quickly out of the Way which I commanded them . . ."
(Exodus 32:8)

They had left *the Way*, the path that God had planned for them. It also signaled a subtle change in relationship between God and His people.

"And the Lord said to Moses, "Go! Go up from here! You and the people that you have brought up out of the land of Egypt, to the land which I swore to Abraham, to Isaac, and to Jacob saying, I shall give it to your seed. And I shall send an angel before you and I shall drive out the Canaanite, the Amorite, the Hittite, the Perizzite, the Hivite, and the Jebusite to a land flowing with milk and honey, for I shall not go up among you so I will not kill you on the way, for you are a stiffnecked people."
(Exodus 33:1–3)

They are now to be led by an angel and *not* God Himself. He was *that* angry with them! That's our God. Remember, we were made in *His* image, so why wouldn't He have emotions too? Of course, He is always in perfect control of them, unlike us! But there's a twist in the tale. Because Moses was able to talk

God round and, with a passionate plea, convinced Him to relent.

> *"And He said, 'My Presence will go with you and I shall give you rest.'"*
> (Exodus 33:14)

And *that's* our God! His Presence was never to leave them over the next few years, indeed *all* they subsequently achieved was because of the very Presence of the Lord Almighty in their midst.

Teachings and bleatings

The Book of Leviticus

This one's had such a bad press perhaps we should call it *Lev-it-alone-icus!* Well, I tried hard to love Leviticus, to declare it as a misunderstood treasure, but, I'm afraid, I failed. It is, quite frankly, for all but the earnest academics and lovers of detail, a little bit boring. It is like the gubbins under the bonnet of a car – important but best left alone by the average Joe. Yet Leviticus is, nevertheless, God's Word and there are oases of insight among the desert sands of tedium. Read on for a few of them.

There's a lot of detail in this book, particularly in reference to the various offerings the Hebrews had to make to Almighty God. Everything had to be done in the right way, following some rigid instructions, with dire penalties for not following the script. There was no slapdash approach permitted, it was serious business.

> *"And the priest that is anointed will take of the bull's blood and bring it to the Tent of Meeting, and the priest will dip his finger in the blood and sprinkle of the blood seven times before the LORD, before the veil of the Sanctuary. And the priest will put some of the blood upon the horns of the altar of sweet incense, which is in the Tent of Meeting before the LORD and will pour all the blood of the bull at the bottom of the altar of*

the burnt offering, which is at the door of the Tent of Meeting. And he will take off from it all the fat of the bull for the sin offering, the fat that covers the innards and all the fat that is upon the innards, the two kidneys and the fat that is upon them, which is by the flanks, and the lobe above the liver with the kidneys, he will take away, as it was taken off from the bull of the offering of peace offerings and the priest will burn them upon the altar of the burnt offering. And the skin of the bull and all its flesh, with its head, with its legs, its innards, and its dung, even the whole bull he will carry forth outside the camp to a clean place, where the ashes are poured out, and burn it on the wood with fire. It will be burned where the ashes are poured out."
(Leviticus 4:5–12)

Yet think of the detailed procedure of say a surgeon, or an airline pilot, where just the slightest deviation could have life-or-death consequences. God was training His people to take Him seriously.

The Bible has a lot of detail whenever He is instructing His people on doing things the right way. It pleased Him that the tabernacle (and later the Temple) was constructed according to His stringent blueprints. It was also important for Him that the Hebrews followed some very detailed and meticulous instructions (more of them later) in the way they lived their lives. To turn that popular saying on its head, *the Deity is in the detail!*

The holiest part of the tabernacle was the *Holy of Holies*, a place visited just once a year, by the High Priest on the Day of Atonement. The only object here was the Ark (box) of the Covenant, a small box just over a metre long, with a gold lid called the *mercy seat*, an interesting name as it's not the *actual* translation of the original Hebrew word, *kapporeth*. This word literally means "the cover" and it's a double meaning. It obviously is the physical cover of the ark, but it is also *the covering*, in the sense of "covering our sins". In other words, it's to do with our atonement. The Greek word used here in the Septuagint (the original Greek translation of the Hebrew

Scriptures) is the word for *propitiation*, a theological term that means "turning away God's justified wrath".

So the mercy seat at the top of the ark in the Holy of Holies was the place where our sins were dealt with and this was where the blood of the sacrifice was applied, seven times on the Day of Atonement. It was at this very place that . . . God dwelt.

> *"The LORD reigns! The peoples will tremble! He is sitting between the cherubim on the Ark. The earth will quake!"*
> (Psalm 99:1)

This was said to be the dwelling place of the *Shekinah glory*, God's visible presence among His people, something that will come to the fore later on in our story, in 1 Kings 8:10–11, when Solomon's temple is consecrated.

> *"And it happened when the priests came out of the Holy Place that the cloud filled the House of the LORD, so that the priests could not stand to minister because of the cloud, because the Glory of the LORD had filled the House of the LORD."*

The idea of God actually dwelling with His people is very Hebraic. God may be different from man, but He's not *remote* from man. This is an active Divine presence, not the "God in the clouds" view that crept into the Church, through the writings of Plato, the Greek philosopher and that achieved its ultimate expression with the *deists* of the 18th and 19th Century, who relegated God to the one who *lit the blue touch-paper* to get all things going then wandered off to allow us to get on with it!

If the mercy seat were lifted one would find three objects inside the ark, as we are told in Hebrews 9:4; Aaron's rod, a pot of manna and the tablets of the Ten Commandments. Arguably all three are symbolic of man's separation from God. How so? Aaron's rod represented the need of a priesthood to mediate between man and God. Manna represented our dependence on God for sustenance. The Ten Commandments represented our natural lawlessness that requires a set of rules to live by.

When God looked down into the ark, He saw these things. But, on the Day of Atonement, when the mercy seat was sprinkled with blood, *this* is what He saw, rather than His separation from man. He saw the blood, the blood of the innocent sacrifice, which *covered* sin and brought reconciliation.

> *"For the life of the flesh is in the blood, and I have given it to you to make atonement for your lives on the altar, for it is the blood that makes atonement for a life."*
> (Leviticus 17:11)

After the details of the various offerings we read about the consecrations of the priests, Aaron and his sons. One interesting feature was the *Urim* (meaning "light") and *Thummim* (meaning "to be made perfect") on the breastplate. These objects functioned to *bring His plans to light*, to help the priests make Godly decisions. We know little of the mechanism here as there is very little light shed on their use elsewhere in the Hebrew Scriptures but one thing suggested here is that God has now started to become quite difficult to hear. Abraham and Moses conversed with Him, as will other individual prophets, but priests, the *middlemen* in God's dealings with man, had to make do with these contraptions. We read in the last chapter that, after the incident with the golden calf, God intended to distance Himself from His people, only convinced otherwise by the pleadings of Moses. Was He losing interest in His people already?

Of course He wasn't, after all, a disinterested Deity wouldn't have appeared thus, after the priests had made the correct offerings:

> *"And Moses and Aaron went in the Tent of Meeting, and came out and blessed the people, then the glory of the LORD appeared to all the people. And a fire came out from before the LORD and consumed the burnt offering*

and the fat on the altar and all the people saw it, and they shouted and fell on their faces."
(Leviticus 9:23–24)

This is the first time the Holy Fire came down to consume the offering. This was an awesome act, made more so by what immediately followed. Two sons of Aaron offered fire of their own making, *strange fire*, and were immediately consumed themselves! Again, this shows us the importance of following God's exact instructions. It was a lesson well learnt.

Other lessons in Leviticus are the various rules and regulations concerning what they were allowed to eat. The accent was always on what was *clean* to eat. God knew best what was good or bad for their bodies and so these instructions were for their own good and not just arbitrary whims. Similarly, the rather detailed instructions that followed, regarding what to do with dead bodies. All very practical and sound advice to avoid infections, something of course they would have known nothing about at that time. Again, God knew best and as always the accent was on *cleanliness*. Over a third of all mentions of the word *clean* in the Bible appear in the Book of Leviticus. After all, the whole purpose of the offerings and sacrifices so meticulously described in this book were *to make His people clean before Him.*

Further along in the book, this theme is summarised when, in a long list of do's and don'ts, there were two situations that God really emphasised:

*"**Do not turn to idols, or make molten gods for yourselves!** I AM the LORD your God!"*
(Leviticus 19:4)

*"**Do not turn to familiar spirits or seek after wizards!** To be defiled by them. I AM the LORD your God!"*
(Leviticus 19:31)

The greatest act of defilement, of losing their cleanliness before Him was in following *other gods*, *spiritism* and *witchcraft*. All activities akin to worshipping the devil himself.

God never changes, unfortunately society does. We may be cleansed by the blood of Christ, but dangers still lurk in the murkiness that surrounds us and regular spring-cleaning is necessary to brush away the dust of the world.

The Book of Numbers

Yes, there *are* a lot of numbers in this book, especially as it starts with a census of the Children of Israel, but the Hebrew name, *B'midbar*, actually means "in the wilderness" and it tells the story of what happened during those forty years or so of wanderings.

In all, 603,550 men started that journey, not including those from the tribe of Levi. The Levites were separated from the rest as they were the ones that *belonged* to God. When the final plague in Egypt had killed off all the first-born sons of the Egyptians, He declared that the first-born sons of the Hebrews *belonged* to Him. Now that the people were a nation, there was to be a "transfer of ownership" to the tribe of Levi, the professional priests. There were 22,000 Levites taking the place of 22,273 first-born sons. The shortfall of 273 was covered by a cash payment to the Levites, a very practical arrangement.

Some Levites had practical duties to fulfil, according to their clans. The Kohath family were to carry the holy objects of the Tabernacle from place to place, the Gershom family carried the curtains and the Merari carried the camping gear, such as the poles and the pegs. But *all* Levites had spiritual duties to perform. And, of course, one must not forget that their very identity was bound up in a very special standing before God.

"And you will set the Levites before Aaron and before his sons and offer them for an offering to the LORD."
(Numbers 8:13)

So not only did they *make* offerings to God, but they themselves *were offerings*, by virtue of the fact that they belonged to
Him. So, not only, as we saw in the last Chapter, were the
offerings themselves – whether burnt, grain, sin or whatever
– meticulously prepared to be acceptable, so also did the Levites
have to be meticulously prepared.

*"And the LORD spoke to Moses saying, "Take the Levites from among the
children of Israel and cleanse them. And you will do thus to them to cleanse
them: Sprinkle purifying water upon them and let them pass a razor over
all their flesh and let them wash their clothes, and so make themselves
clean. Then let them take a young bull with its grain offering, fine flour
mixed with oil, and you will take another young bull for a sin offering.
And you will bring the Levites in front of the Tent of Meeting and you
will gather the whole assembly of the children of Israel together, and
you will bring the Levites before the LORD, and the children of Israel will
put their hands upon the Levites. And Aaron will offer the Levites before
the LORD, a wave offering of the children of Israel, so they can execute the
service of the LORD. And the Levites will lay their hands upon the heads
of the bulls and you will offer one, a sin offering, and the other a burnt
offering, to the LORD, to make atonement for the Levites. And you will set
the Levites before Aaron and before his sons and offer them for an offering
to the LORD. Thus you will separate the Levites from among the children
of Israel and the Levites will be Mine."*
(Numbers 8:5–14)

If the book of Leviticus could be encapsulated into that
single word, "cleanliness", then perhaps the book of Numbers
could do the same for something a little more negative. There's
a sad refrain, repeated many times, of the people *complaining,
grumbling, kvetching*! It's troubling, as we shall see, because the
consequences are deadly! Here's an example:

*"And the people were complaining: it displeased the LORD and the LORD
heard it, and His anger was kindled and the fire of the LORD burned*

among them and consumed those that were in the outermost parts of the camp."
(Numbers 11:1)

Oh dear, didn't they know who they were dealing with? But then you look at the context and you realise that their behaviour had fallen well below God's exacting standards. They were cavorting about lustfully and moaning about the *manna*, remembering the meat, cucumbers, melons and leeks that they enjoyed as slaves in Egypt. Moses listened to this sorry bunch and decided that it was all too much for him. *"Lord"*, he cried, *"for how much longer am I to carry these people?"*

God grants him his wish and he granted the people their wish. For Moses He allows him to appoint seventy elders to help shoulder the responsibility. To the others He says, *"You want meat, then I'll give you meat! In fact I'll give you so much meat it will come out of your nostrils and you'll begin to hate the taste of it!"*

And to show them He meant business, He poured His Spirit over those elders so that a mini-charismatic revival took place and they prophesised all over the place. And as for the rest, He provided quails to eat, then, while they were scoffing the meat, inflicted all of those who had disgraced themselves earlier, with a plague that killed them!

God was not to be mocked.

There followed another sorry episode, with a far more tragic consequence. It was the report from the spies sent out to survey the "Promised Land". *There be giants there*, declared the bad spies, provoking the moaning masses to start pining for the security of Egypt and querying God's motives. Do they not learn?

Thank goodness for the two good and honest spies, Joshua and Caleb, who spoke the truth of *a land of milk and honey* and emphatically urged the people not to rebel against God and certainly *not to be in awe* of the people who currently lived there.

But God was looking on in anger and threatening to wipe them out but Moses intervenes and His anger diminishes. Then, offering both forgiveness and judgement, He declares:

"And the LORD said, 'I have pardoned according to your word. But as truly as I live, all the earth will be filled with the glory of the LORD. Because all those men who have seen My glory and My miracles, which I did in Egypt and in the wilderness and have tested Me now these ten times, and have not hearkened to My voice. Surely they will not see the land which I swore to their fathers, neither will any of them who provoked Me see it.'"
(Numbers 14:20–23)

There followed forty years of wandering in the wilderness and the only people to reach the *Land of Milk and Honey* were to be Joshua, Caleb and the children of their generation.

Again, God was not to be mocked.

But the moaning and grumbling still doesn't end and Korah, a couple of his mates and 250 others rebel against Moses, challenging his authority before God. Moses is angry and upset and so is God, who urges Moses to divide up the people into the pro-Moses and anti-Moses factions, keeping them well apart and emphatically declaring, *do not touch anything of theirs lest you be consumed in all their sins!*

He was going to make an example of these rebels and rather than just smiting them with a plague, He caused the ground literally to swallow up Korah and his two friends, as well as their houses and belongings and a fire to consume the 250 rebels!

The very next day, believe it or not, many were still complaining, blaming Moses and Aaron for killing *the people of the LORD*. A self-inflicted death sentence, no less! God unleashed a plague that raged through the whole congregation, stopped only by the actions of Aaron, who offered an atoning sacrifice for the people. Not before 14,700 had perished!

Yet again, God was not to be mocked.

Once and for all, the authority of Moses and Aaron was confirmed through the budding of Aaron's staff. This became an emblem of God's provisions and was eventually kept in the Ark of the Covenant as a testimony.

But the bad behaviour still continued and it wasn't confined to that first generation who were denied their destiny. No, it also affected their children, the very people who were granted the inheritance of the "Promised Land". They were in the land of the Moabites, to the east and Moses' days were almost over.

"And Israel stayed in Acacia and the people began to commit harlotry with the daughters of Moab. And they called the people to the sacrifices of their gods and the people did eat and bow down to their gods. And Israel joined himself to Baal Peor, and the anger of the LORD was kindled against Israel."
(Numbers 25:1–3)

Would you credit it!? So near yet . . . so far. This sorry episode even got a mention in Paul's letter to the Corinthians (1 Corinthians 10:9), because no less than 24,000 perished in the resultant plague, a number that would have been larger if it weren't for the actions of Phineas, the grandson of Aaron, who dispatched one particularly cocky miscreant and his lover with a javelin. (As an aside, there is a white supremacist group called the *Phineas Priesthood* who take this episode as their model for inter-racial hatred. They are fiercely anti-Semitic, have an aversion to paying tax and are designated as a terrorist group. It's amazing how people still wrestle Bible stories out of their context and mangle their meanings to fit in with whatever they want to claim is God-approved!)

And, yes, God is still not to be mocked and this time, He deals also with the enemy, those Midianites living in the land of Moab, who were mainly responsible for corrupting His people. It was to be the last major act in Moses' life.

"And the LORD *spoke to Moses, saying, "Avenge the children of Israel of the Midianites: afterward you will be gathered to your people."*
(Numbers 31:1–2)

They slaughtered all of the men and took the women and children into captivity. But this wasn't enough, because surely it was many of these very women who had led the Hebrews astray. So they were killed too, the only ones spared being the virgins, who plainly bore no responsibility.

This has been a bloodthirsty chapter and we know that there is more to come once the Children of Israel start conquering the land. It makes us uncomfortable and many Christians go into denial, finding it impossible to countenance such an angry God. Yet the stories are here in God's Word, alongside the nicer "Sunday School" fare of manna in the desert and parting seas.

We have to accept that there are things that God knows that we can't even get close to understanding. It's our desire for wisdom and understanding that gets us into such positions. Rather than having faith in God's actions and motives we use our rational processes to judge Him by whatever standards are *en vogue* in the culture in which we live.

Perhaps it becomes easier to understand if we again consider the major theme of the previous book, Leviticus, the need for *cleanliness*. This theme continues. Cleanliness was expected *in mind*, through the detailed list of procedures that had to be followed in the tabernacle and *in body*, through the meticulous dietary and social laws. But what about *in spirit*? God is trying to purify His people who were, after all, meant to be a kingdom of priests. And how do you do this, knowing that, in those times, once sin had gripped the heart there was not much chance of a release? If people persisted in breaking the first two of His Commandments – the ones concerning idols and other gods – then, for the good of the whole, they had to be pruned, otherwise the blight was going to spread. God had to know *who were really **His** people*.

This ragtag band of people were on the verge of invading a land teeming with militarily-experienced foes, who had been entrenched in the land for generations and were not going to give up the "Land of Milk and Honey" without a fight. Do you really think they had the slightest chance of success *if God wasn't going to fight their battles for them?*

And God was only going to do so if He could be sure that they were *wholeheartedly* His people. That's why pruning was necessary.

The Book of Deuteronomy

Well, the name says it all, both in English and in Hebrew. In English, *Deuteronomy* derives from the Greek word meaning "second law" and, in Hebrew, *Devarim*, simply means "words". The vast majority of the book are the *words* of Moses, speaking in Moab just before the *push westwards* to the Promised Land. And these words are basically re-iterating the Torah, the teachings, of Moses; in essence it is the teachings (law) given for a *second time*. So, what can we learn from it, seeing that we've already covered most of the material in the previous three Books of Moses?

Sometimes we need reminders of important things. The Children of Israel certainly did. First he reminds them of their mission that is bound up in their very destiny:

> "*Look, I have set the land before you: Go in! Possess the land which the* LORD *swore to your fathers, Abraham, Isaac, and Jacob, to give to them and to their seed after them!*"
> (Deuteronomy 1:8)

He re-iterates this in verse 21, with emphasis:

> "*Behold, the* LORD *your God has set the land before you. Go up! Possess it! As the* LORD *God of your fathers has said to you,* **'Do not be in awe! Do not be dismayed!'**"

He stresses that they should not be in awe of their enemies as God will be fighting their battles for them, even meddling with the minds of the enemy kings, as He did with Pharaoh!

> *"But Sihon king of Heshbon would not let us pass by him, for the* Lord *your God strengthened his spirit and made his heart obstinate, so He could deliver him into your hand as on this day."*
> (Deuteronomy 2:30)

There's an interesting little snippet that I had always thought was only voiced in the Book of Revelation. It is this:

> *"You will not add to the word which I command you, neither will you take anything from it, so you can keep the commandments of the* Lord *your God which I command you."*
> (Deuteronomy 4:2)

This one can open up a whole bag of hot potatoes! A warning to those who add to the Torah, but also to those who conveniently skip over a few of the harder commandments. Is this just for Moses' brethren, or for Jews today also? And what about Christians, both Jews and Gentiles? You may ponder on this, if you wish, but this one's for a future book!

Moses then begins reminding people of these commandments, with the greatest stress on the need to avoid idolatry, followed by the *Ten Commandments*. The verse that follows remains *the most revered piece of Scripture* for Jews from that day to now:

> *"Listen! Obey, O Israel! The* Lord *is our God! The* Lord *is One! And you will love the* Lord *your God with all your heart, with your very being, and with all your might."*
> (Deuteronomy 6:4–5)

This is the Sh'ma and proclaims not only the centrality of God in our lives, but expects us to act accordingly, to *obey* once we have listened (something missed by most other Bible trans-lations that start with the words, *Hear, O Israel!*). Jewish martyrs have died with this prayer on their lips and it is recited at every synagogue service, even at most "messianic" fellowships, also as a final prayer shared by parent and child at bedtime.

These words are to be proclaimed in a whole variety of circumstances, as we read the rest of the passage:

> *"And these words, which I am commanding you this day, will be in your heart and you will teach them diligently to your children, and you will talk of them when you sit in your house, when you walk by the way, when you lie down, and when you rise up. And you will bind them as a sign upon your hand, and they will be as frontlets between your eyes. And you will write them on the doorposts of your house and on your gates."*
> (Deuteronomy 6:6–9)

The thrust of this is to make the Sh'ma known universally, to your children, at home and on your travels. What has happened is that these commands have been taken literally, in the form of *tefillin* (where the scripture is inside boxes held together on the forehead and forearm by leather straps) and the *mezuzah* (where the scripture is inside a tiny ornate casing on the doorpost).

Without demeaning these practices, I can't help feeling that this wasn't the original point, from God's perspective. *Tefillin* is a visible mark of the ritual of an orthodox Jew and the *mezuzah* is a sign of a Jewish presence in a household. Yet *these words* are hidden inside boxes and are not displayed as a witness to our God, something that the first half of the passage is posi-tively screaming for us to do. The message is clear. *This is a central message and we should do all that we can to proclaim it!*

As I write this, it is the month of November and a lot of men are walking around with hastily grown moustaches. It is a response to a national health campaign called *Movember*. So what message is being proclaimed here? That growing moustaches is good for your health? No, the actual campaign is for awareness of prostate and testicular cancer, but I don't see the connection. Of course, if the moustache was in a relevant area of the body . . . but then no-one would see it anyway! The point is that only those in the know would relate moustache growing to prostate cancer.

In the same way, only those familiar already with Deuteronomy 6:4–5 would equate *tefillin* and *mezuzahs* with the Scripture that lay within. Of course, Scripture is Scripture and the verses seem to be asking to be taken literally, but I'm thinking how more effective it would be if *the Scripture itself* were displayed on the door frames and on the forehead (not sure how, though). Just a thought.

Here's another thought of a practical nature. Shouldn't we thank God (say grace) *after* meals?

> *". . . When you have eaten and are full, watch out for yourselves so you do not forget the Lord."*
> (Deuteronomy 6:11–12)

> *"When you have eaten and are full, then you will bless the Lord your God for the good land which He has given you."*
> (Deuteronomy 8:10)

Just another thought.

Deuteronomy is very much a *re-iteration* book, with Moses reminding the people of what is important for them to stay a holy, separate people. It appears that memories were short as God reminded them over thirty times in this book alone that He had rescued them from slavery in Egypt. And why did He rescue them?

> *"The Lord did not set His love upon you, nor choose you because you were more in number than any people, for you were the fewest of all people, but because the Lord loved you and because He would keep the*

*oath which He had sworn to your fathers, the LORD has brought you out
with a mighty hand and redeemed you from the house of bondage, from
the hand of Pharaoh king of Egypt."*
(Deuteronomy 7:7–8)

God doesn't forget His promises. Then there's the difficult
bit (for us), the manner of the task that lay ahead.

*"And you will consume all the peoples that the LORD your God will deliver
to you. Your eye will have no pity upon them, neither will you serve their
gods, for that will be a snare to you. If you will say in your heart, 'These
nations are more than I, how can I dispossess them?' You will not be
afraid of them, but will well remember what the LORD your God did to
Pharaoh and to all Egypt."*
(Deuteronomy 7:16–18)

And again He reminds them about the manner of the coming
victories:

*"Understand therefore this day that the LORD your God is He Who Goes
Over Before You. He will destroy them like a consuming fire, and He will
bring them down before your face so you will drive them out and destroy
them quickly, as the LORD has said to you."*
(Deuteronomy 9:3)

And what did the Children of Israel have to do?

*"Circumcise therefore the foreskin of your heart, and no longer be stiff
necked."*
(Deuteronomy 10:16)

Well, that's a surprise, we thought that this was a *New
Testament* principle (Romans 2:29)? It's stated even more clearly
later on, talking of a future time when the outward sign had
to be matched by an inward conviction.

"And the LORD *your God will circumcise your heart and the heart of your descendants, to love the* LORD *your God with all your heart and with your whole being, so you may live."*
(Deuteronomy 30:6)

Moses then lays out the central part of his message, which is going to define the destiny of these people, right up to modern times. He grabs their attention with the first word, then expounds:

*"**Behold**! I* AM *setting before you this day a blessing and a curse; a blessing, if you obey the commandments of the* LORD *your God, which I command you this day and a curse, if you will not obey the commandments of the* LORD *your God, but turn aside out of the Way which I command you this day, to go after other gods, which you have not known."*
(Deuteronomy 11:26–28)

To receive blessings and not curses, all they had to do was to stay in *the Way*, which, as we have already seen, is all about actions, deeds and works, practical applications flowing from their love of God.

God lays it out even clearer in Deuteronomy 30:15–20:

"See, I have set before you this day life and good, and death and evil; in that I command you this day to love the LORD *your God, to walk in His Ways, and to keep His commandments and His statutes and His judgments, so you will live and multiply. And the* LORD *your God will bless you in the land where you go to possess it. But if your heart turns away, so that you will not heed, but will be drawn away and worship other gods, and serve them; I announce to you this day that you will surely perish, you will not prolong your days upon the land which you cross the Jordan to go to possess it. I'll call heaven and earth to witness this day against you, I have set before you life and death, blessing and cursing. Therefore **choose life**, so both you and your descendants may live, so you can love the* LORD *your God, so you can obey His voice and you can cleave to Him,*

for He is your life and the length of your days, so you can stay in the land
which the LORD swore to give to Abraham, Isaac and Jacob."

Biblical and secular history shows us that they didn't make
a good choice. Deuteronomy Chapter 28 shows us both what
blessings they lost and what curses they heaped on their heads,
often told with stark chilling details. A story of centuries of
anti-Semitism, *told in advance!*

The Book ends with the Song of Moses, which he spoke and
taught to the Children of Israel. No pleasant ode to their
greatness, or rhapsody of coming triumphs, but rather a litany
of criticism, judgement and dire prophecy.

"They forsook God Who made them, and lightly esteemed the Rock of
their Salvation. They provoked Him to jealousy with strange gods; with
abominations they provoked Him to anger. They sacrificed to demons,
not to God, to gods whom they did not know, to new gods that recently
came up, whom your fathers did not dread. You are unmindful of the
Rock that begot you and have forgotten God Who formed you. "And
the LORD saw it and abhorred them because of the provoking of His sons
and of His daughters. "
(Deuteronomy 32:15–19)

This is an interesting passage, but not obviously so. The interesting part is the various *different* Names it uses for God. Here
it is again, with Names inserted (in bold):

*"They forsook **Eloah** Who made them, and lightly esteemed the Rock of*
their Salvation. They provoked Him to jealousy with strange gods; with
abominations they provoked Him to anger. They sacrificed to demons,
*not to **Elah**, to **elohim** whom they did not know, to new gods that recently*
came up, whom your fathers did not dread. You are unmindful of the
*Rock that begot you and have forgotten El Who formed you. "And **YHWH***
saw it and abhorred them because of the provoking of His sons and of
His daughters. "

When reading Scripture in English we often miss the subtleties of the writing, expressed with this amazing, evocative language called Hebrew. And one of the best examples of this is when God Himself is referenced. Here we see five variations, falling into two groups. The first is based around the Hebrew word *El* and the second is the tetragrammaton (Greek word meaning "four letters"), *YHWH*.

The Hebrew word *El* has an interesting history. One of the earliest words known to man, it appeared in pre-history as a Proto-Canaanite word, formed from two pictures, that of an ox's head and that of a staff or a crook. The idea to be conveyed was of leadership or strength (from the ox's head) and of a guiding hand (from the crook). So, the original word gives the sense of "strong guided leadership", an apt, though simplistic, description of God's function. This developed into the Hebrew letters *aleph* and *lamed*, producing the word *El*. (For more details on this you may want to read my book, *God's Signature*.)

El is the generic title for God and appears over 200 times in the Hebrew Scriptures, with around 20 of these referring to a "god" other than the *real* God. The variation *Eloah* conveys the idea of a mighty powerful One and appears a lot in the Book of Job. Its plural is *Elohim*, a word that appears over 2,500 times and is the Hebrew word that lies behind most uses of the word "God" in Scripture. It is not His personal Name, it is just a description of His function. To illustrate:

*"**In the beginning** God created the heavens and the earth."*
(Genesis 1:1)

The word used for "God" here is *Elohim*, God displaying His power in the Creation.

"And the LORD God formed man from the dust of the ground and blew into his nostrils the breath of life, and man became a living being."
(Genesis 2:7)

Here God is still creating, hence the use of *Elohim*, but now it is used in conjunction with a new word, LORD. This is YHWH, God's *personal Name*. This is because, in the narrative, we now start to see Him in communion with man, so it starts to become more personal.

An interesting point is that, in the interaction with Eve in the garden, the serpent/Satan reverts to the *impersonal* Elohim, avoiding addressing God by His Name.

The other name used for God in the Deuteronomy passage is *Elah*. This is curious, as it is an Aramaic variation, used mostly in the Books of Ezra and Daniel. Everything in God's word is for a purpose, so its inclusion in this one place in Deuteronomy must have a purpose, too. Perhaps one of you dear readers can investigate this one as a bit of homework?

Finally, also hidden within the Song of Moses is a promise for the future:

"They have moved Me to jealousy with that which is not God. They have provoked Me to anger with their vanities and I shall move them to jealousy with those who are not a people."
(Deuteronomy 32:21)

Those who are not a people? Yes, the Gentiles are coming . . . but not yet.

Trouble and strife

CHAPTER

3

The Book of Joshua

It was time to cash in on the promise. The battalions were organised, the soldiers trained for battle, the tanks greased up, all weapons loaded and primed. Well that's how invasions are *usually* planned . . . but not in this case. All the Children of Israel needed was trust in their leader, Joshua. And all *he* needed was trust in his God. Easier said than done and a lot of reassurances were needed: *Be strong! Be of good courage!* (Joshua 1:6). *Only be strong! Be very courageous!* (Joshua 1:7). *Be strong! Be of good courage!* **Do not tremble! Do not be dismayed!** (Joshua 1:9).

God had a very direct way to assure Joshua that his army would be right behind him:

> *"Whoever he is who rebels against your command and will not heed your words in all that you command him, he will be put to death: only be strong and of good courage!"*
> (Joshua 1:18)

The thing is that, as has already been said, this was to be no ordinary military campaign. It was going to be no less than *one big mighty act of God*, with Joshua and his army as willing instruments to this end. All that was needed was perfect understanding and communication between the two parties. They were really going to have to do everything God asked and *never question His orders.*

The first campaign was before them, *Jericho.* Total destruction was called for. Only one family was to be spared, that of Rahab (the harlot?), saved by her faith and the scarlet cord bound on the window, just as the Exodus generation were saved by their faith and the scarlet blood on their doorposts. There's a pattern there, perhaps we will see it repeated? Another pattern is given by the miraculous river crossing that preceded it, reminiscent of the incident at the Sea.

"And the priests who carried the Ark of the Covenant of the LORD stood firm on dry ground in the middle of the Jordan, and all Israel crossed over on dry ground, until all the people had completely crossed over the Jordan." (Joshua 3:17)

It was as if new chapters in God's dealings with his people were to be *heralded in by a miracle.* Reminiscent of Jesus' earthly life (starting with the virgin birth) and the birth of the Church (as a result of the Resurrection and the giving of the Spirit).

God's new dealings with the Israelites, as they began the invasion, were to be accompanied by signs. First they celebrated the Passover, then manna ceased on the very next day. The men were circumcised, a practice that had ceased in the wilderness, perhaps because they had had enough other hardships to contend with there!

It wasn't the trumpets that brought down the walls of Jericho, it was the shouts, after six days of shofar-blowing:

"And it was at the seventh time when the priests blew with the shofars, Joshua said to the people, Shout! The LORD has given you the city!" (Joshua 6:16)

But it wasn't every wall that crumbled, the part left standing was the section that housed Rahab and her family. Then Jericho was totally destroyed, apart from silver, gold and vessels of bronze and iron. Every *accursed* thing was destroyed . . . except for one, a *cloak of Shinar*, smuggled out by a foolish man called Achan. He paid dearly for this act, a direct disobedience of God's command, that brought judgement on Israel (in the form of 36 men dying needlessly in battle) as well as his whole family, all killed.

All because of *one accursed thing*. A point was being made here, that just a single act was enough to bring judgement on all. An act against God was an act against the *whole community*, something a little alien to us in our individualistic times. Community was extremely important to the Children of Israel.

Achan's act in stealing *that accursed thing* was to make him *that accursed man* and, until his sin was made public, rendered the Hebrews into *that accursed nation*. That was until he was discovered and redemption was made through his death. As with many other occasions in their journey from Egypt so far, this was an uncomfortable truth and a tough learning process in living out the words of their promise before Moses and God at the foot of Sinai:

"And Moses went up to God. And the LORD *called to him out of the mountain saying, 'Thus will you say to the House of Jacob and tell the children of Israel. You have seen what I did to the Egyptians, how I bore you on eagles' wings, and brought you to Myself. Now therefore, if you will indeed obey My voice and keep My covenant, then you will be a peculiar treasure to Me above all people, for all the earth is Mine. And you will be a kingdom of priests to Me and a holy nation. These are the words which you will speak to the children of Israel.' And Moses came and called for the elders of the people and laid before them all these words which the* LORD *commanded him. And all the people answered together and said, 'All that the* LORD *has spoken we will do.'"*
(Exodus 19:3–8)

A kingdom of priests and a holy nation. They had to keep themselves *pure and clean*, as we have already discussed. They must not be tainted by the nations that surrounded them! This was serious stuff. This was an enormous responsibility that they took on. If they had realised this, generations earlier at the foot of Sinai, then perhaps they wouldn't have signed up so readily. It's not plain sailing being the *chosen people*, you know!

This was all a bit of a shock to poor old Joshua. He again needed assurances. After all, they were now ready for battle for the *second time* against Ai. The first time had brought defeat and the death of 36 men, thanks to Achan's concealed sin. God reassures him:

"And the LORD *said to Joshua,* **Do not in any way be awed! Do not be dismayed!** *Take all the people of war with you and rise! Go up to Ai! See, I have given the king of Ai, his people, his city, and his land into your hand."*
(Joshua 8:1)

Victory came, resulting in the destruction of the city, the slaughter of 12,000 and the King of Ai hung on a tree then left as a sign at the gates of the city. You don't mess with the God of Israel!

Joshua used this occasion to remind his people of the facts of life for them. He built an altar and then read aloud the whole Torah to the complete assembly, reminding them of the blessings and curses therein.

This was important because the Kings of the nations had now fully taken notice and were beginning to plot and plan and build alliances. The serious stuff was about to start. Game on . . .

Adoni-Zedek, the King of Jerusalem was one such king who made alliances with four other nations to attack Gibeon, who had (through trickery) just made peace with the Israelites. He obviously hadn't read God's script:

"And the LORD *said to Joshua,* **Do not be in awe of them!** *I have delivered them into your hand. Not a man of them will stand before you."*
(Joshua 10:8)

Their armies were slaughtered, more from hailstones slung down from heaven than by the swords of the Israelites. And to give Joshua a bit more time to finish them off, God obliged by causing the sun and moon to stay still, to give them a bit of extra light!

There followed more such battles and victories, all the time God reassuring His people not to be in awe, but to trust Him. We *too* must trust Him on this. We must truly trust that His motives are perfect and that, when we can't fathom Him out, the fault is not with Him, but with our *lack of understanding* of Him. The fact is that the battles were necessary, as was the level of destruction, in order to maintain a separation between God's people and the pagan ideas that surrounded them, ideas that had developed over many generations and that surely must have tried His patience. This is not an *unloving* God Who ordered the destruction of so many people, but rather Someone who knew the bigger picture, Who was in fact the *Creator* of the bigger picture, who always acts at the right moment and tempers justice with mercy, even when we can't see it because He hasn't seen fit to explain all of His actions to us.

You get the impression of a drama being acted out, with more going on than we realise. There were unseen battles too, as you would hardly expect the devil to allow God's plans to unfold without attempts to *thwart the said plans*. Yes, there was a drama indeed acting out, over the future of God's *chosen people*. Yet it was a drama with only *one* possible ending. This is made clear in Joshua 11:20:

> *"For it was of the* LORD *to harden their hearts, so they would come against Israel in battle, so he could utterly destroy them, so they might have no favor, but that He might destroy them, as the* LORD *commanded Moses."*

And that's what happened until we read, three verses later, *and the land rested from war.*

The land was then divided up and granted to the tribes of the Israelites (apart from the Levites, who were given 48 cities to live in) and the tabernacle set up in Shiloh.

There's one last story that is worth recounting. It concerned the three tribes who were given land to the east of the Jordan river. They had built *their own altar*, an act that invoked dangerous memories of when the Israelites were caught cavorting with the Midianite women not much earlier. That particular act brought terrible judgement upon the whole of Israel and of course the Achan episode was still in living memory. So the other tribes met at Shiloh planning to go to war against them.

It turned out that sometimes words are preferable to actions and Phineas was first sent to chat with them. He discovered that their motives were of the purest, they simply wanted to worship God and provide a witness to Him and it was just too much of a *schlep* to cross the river to visit Shiloh, the officially sanctioned place of worship. This explanation was accepted and that altar was given the name "witness", *for it will be a witness between us that the* LORD *is God* (Joshua 22:34).

Perhaps we too are quick to judge when other Christians start a new work that is unfamiliar to us and our "discernment radar" starts tingling. We are not to be the ones to judge, as God may truly be doing a *new thing*. Instead we must watch, pray and examine the fruit and only then, if necessary, act. The last thing we would want to do is to oppose the work of the Holy Spirit in other people's lives, however strange their activities may seem to us.

We leave this book on a high note (despite a few final warnings by Joshua, just before his death).

"And Israel served the LORD *all the days of Joshua and all the days of the elders who lived long after Joshua and had known all the works of the* LORD, *that He had done for Israel."*
(Joshua 24:31)

The Book of Judges

Let's start with a recap. In fulfilment of a promise given hundreds of years earlier to Abraham and his family, God rescues their descendants from slavery in Egypt and forges them into a nation. This was a troublesome, argumentative bunch and, despite witnessing miracle after miracle and accepting the mandate of a *kingdom of priests*, they constantly moaned, rebelled and, at key moments, failed to put total trust in Moses, who led them and God Himself, Who *really* led them. This doomed the first generation to forty years of unfulfilled wanderings in the wilderness. It was their children, led by Joshua, one of only a few righteous survivors of that generation, who were to inherit the "Promised Land".

Yet this was a flawed generation too and they almost never made it across the Jordan, saved only by the actions of Phineas, who put a stop to some unseemly cavorting with the Midianite women. Despite a good start to the military campaign, with the destruction of Jericho, the actions of Achan showed that they weren't 100% God-fearing. God made it clear that the Land was only going to be conquered if they were 100% behind Him, which would ensure that He was 100% before them in their battles. This was demonstrated again and again with the military successes that were to follow and we reach the end of Joshua's life with the land conquered . . . for the time being. But Joshua knew, as did Moses before him, that this story was not going to have a happy ending . . .

The book of Judges explains why and can basically be summarised thus:

> When Israel listened to God all was well, but when they fell away they were shown the consequences of their sin (usually through matters of war), which prompted them to cry out to God, who sent them a Judge, who led them back to listening to Him.

It all started with a rebuke from an angel of the Lord (arguably Jesus himself), reminding them of the covenant with Abraham that gave them the land, but how they were treading on *dangerous territory* by making their own covenants with the pagan nations. He then made the following judgement against them:

> *"I shall not drive them out from before you, but they will be as thorns in your sides and their gods will be a snare to you."*
> (Judges 2:3)

At this they wept! And so they should, because we are told that this was a generation *that did not know the LORD or even the works He had done for Israel.*

Before we make our own judgements here, perhaps we too could learn from this. The Christian Church was also meant to be a *kingdom of priests*, a holy and separate people, living God-centred lives and unsullied by the ways of the world, with its alternative lifestyles, philosophies and false gods. Yet God, in His wisdom, has allowed us to tread similar paths to those Israelites. From the 2nd Century AD, when Greek philosophy was allowed to gain a foothold in the Western Church, we too have had our *heads turned* by the world and, rather than dishing out the extreme penalties suffered by those Israelites who turned away from Him, He has allowed these "alternatives" to be *thorns in our sides and a snare to us.*

How much has the Church sold out to the world? (for a thorough examination of this, you may want to read my book, *The Bishop's New Clothes*). Do we know that the world has provided snares for us? The tragedy is that, by and large, we don't. We desperately need Judges, as in those earlier times, to bring us back to the fold. There have been some who have done this, men such as John Wesley or Billy Graham. But where are the judges for our current generation?

"Nevertheless the LORD raised judges who delivered them out of the hand of those who plundered them. And yet they would not listen to their judges, but they went astray after other gods and bowed themselves to them. They turned quickly from the Way in which their fathers walked, obeying the commandments of the LORD, but they did not do so."
(Judges 2:16–17)

Again we see *the Way of the Lord*, the way in which we must live, as detailed in the Torah for that generation and from the whole counsel of God, in ours. How easily we (and they) forget the ancient paths.

There were around a dozen judges sent by the Lord, men (and a woman) anointed for this role by the Spirit of God. There was *Othniel, Ehud* of the withered hand and *Shamgar*, who slew 600 men with a pointy stick. There was *Deborah* (helped by the brave Jael and her tent peg) and, of course, *Gideon*. He started his mission by destroying his father's altar to Baal, an act for which he was almost killed (which shows you how far the Israelites had fallen!) With just 300 men he defeated the whole Midianite army, an episode that showed that the Lord God was fighting for them and could have achieved the same ends if it had been just Gideon and his mother-in-law confronting the enemy. *The sword for the LORD and for Gideon*, cried the 300 as the army numbering in their thousands fled before them!

Then there was *Tola* and *Jair*, who led them for twenty two years. This was followed, according to the pattern, by a period of rebellion and anarchy. We read, in Judges 10:6, how low they had got:

"Then the children of Israel again brought anarchy in the sight of the LORD and served baalim and Ashtarot, the gods of Syria, the gods of Sidon, the gods of Moab, the gods of the children of Ammon, and the gods of the Philistines and forsook the LORD, and did not serve Him."

God's judgement for this was to sell them into the hands of the Ammonites and the Philistines. The next judge was *Jephthah*, followed by Ibzan, Elon, Avdon. Then came *Samson*.

Ah, Samson, proof that God doesn't just pick the goody-goodies to represent Him! The children's story books fail to mention that he was a fiery, vengeful, fornicating thug, whose personal kill-count numbered in the thousands, including a lion. Yet he was a judge for twenty years and was born to a scenario reminiscent of Abraham and Sarah (barren mother) and also Joseph and Mary (visited by an angel – arguably Jesus himself in this case – and told how special their son would be). So, if his entrance into this world was memorable, then his exit was epic! Betrayed by his conniving nag of a wife, he was shorn of his hair (the source of his great strength), blinded and taken to the temple of Dagon, where he was forced to entertain the Philistines (that's what the Hebrew word actually says – he made them laugh). So he possibly did a stand-up comedy routine and for an encore stood by the main pillars of the temple and *brought the house down*!

The book ends on a sad note:

> *"In those days there was no king in Israel: each man did what was right in his own eyes."*
> (Judges 21:25)

Will things get better, or worse? Well, we will soon see them getting better . . . and then much worse!

The Book of Ruth

But first a short interlude, with this famous little story that inhabits the times of the Judges. It's a beautiful tale and is used to illustrate the future relationship between Gentiles and Jews within the Church. Yet, at the same time it is troubling.

Now the Nation of Israel has been called the "wife" of God, in the sense of the covenant made at Sinai and the Book of

Deuteronomy has been said to be the *marriage contract*. This has also been drawn out in a prophetic sense in the Book of Hosea. If we continue in this vein and consider *Christians*, who are of course known as the Bride of Christ, we can stretch this whole metaphor and realise that Israel is the *mother-in-law* of the Church! And who *truly* gets on with their mother-in-law? That's 2,000 years of "Christian anti-Semitism" explained by a metaphor!

Ruth was a Gentile from the hated nation of Moab. Naomi was Ruth's Jewish mother-in-law and here was a relationship that went against the grain of the common stereotype of friction between two ladies with a common man in their life. Ruth was the dream daughter-in-law and proved the means for not only Naomi's physical survival but also for her happiness, in the form of Ruth's baby, which became *their* baby (as well as King David's grandfather).

But is this true of the way the Gentile Church has treated *its* mother-in-law? Not really, in fact the story has been very different, with the Church generally withholding any understanding of salvation (through Jesus) from its Jewish *mother-in-law*. Has the Church honestly been seen acting out these words?

> *"Your people are my people, and your God is my God. Where you die, I shall die and there I shall be buried: the* Lord *do so to me, more also, if anything but death part you and me."*
> (Ruth 1:16–17)

The story of Ruth has not yet had its prophetic fulfilment, but that doesn't mean that it never will. It just means that the Gentile Church needs to read this important little story again and ask what God is calling it *and you* to do, whether you are male or female, to bring this story to a happy conclusion.

Take two Kings

The First Book of Samuel

Here is where we meet *the Lord of Hosts* (YHWH Zeba'ot) for the first time.

> *"And this man went up out of his city yearly to worship and to sacrifice to the Lord of Hosts in Shiloh . . ."*
> (1 Samuel 1:3)

This gives us an image of God as the commander of a great heavenly army of angels and, indeed, in 1 Samuel 17:45 we get confirmation of this:

> *". . . I come to you in the name of the Lord of Hosts, the God of the armies of Israel . . ."*

This majestic title appears over 200 times in the Hebrew Scriptures and we will meet it again later on in our story.

Closed wombs seem to occur quite a lot in the Bible. We already know about Sarah, Rachel and Samson's mother and we are about to meet a new one, *Hannah*. One thing they all have in common is that the fruit of their womb, a firstborn son, is to be a very special person. Hannah was a virtuous woman, who prayed that, if God would give her a son then she would give him back to God. Her faith was such that, once the prayer was over, *her countenance was no longer sad*, because she knew that God would answer her.

Samuel was the answer and, as he trained for the priesthood, he was also the answer to the pertinent question, *what are we going to do with Eli the priest and particularly his sons?* These sons were wicked men, stealing food meant for sacrificing, threatening those who resisted and sleeping with women outside the tabernacle. They either didn't know, or didn't care that *God is not to be mocked*. They'd as good as signed their death warrants!

A *proper* man of God came to Eli and proclaimed:

> *"And this will be a sign to you that will come upon your two sons, on Hophni and Phineas, in one day both of them will die, and I shall raise up for Myself a faithful priest, who will do according to what is in My heart and in My mind, and I shall build him a sure house and he will walk before My anointed forever."*
> (1 Samuel 2:34–35)

As a result of these errant priests, *the word of the LORD was rare in those days. There was no frequent vision.* (1 Samuel 3:1). That was until God appeared to Samuel, *and the LORD said to Samuel, Behold, I AM doing a thing in Israel at which both the ears of everyone who hears will tingle* (1 Samuel 3:11).

Samuel became the man for his times, a prophet of the LORD. He had his work cut out, because the next thing we read is how the Israelites foolishly took the Ark of the Covenant with them, as they fought the Philistines and managed to get it captured (there is good news here, as Eli's evil sons were killed in the process, as was Eli himself when he heard the news, falling off a gate and breaking his neck). But the story doesn't end there, actually it takes a bit of a comic turn. The Ark is placed next to the pagan idol of Dagon, which gets knocked over and its hands drop off. Then, wherever the Philistines take the Ark, men developed piles (or were killed) and ended up returning it on a cart strapped to two milk cows, containing an offering of golden piles!

Soon the Israelites began to look at the nations around them. These people had *Kings*, who led them into battle, ruled them, made decisions for them. *We want a King, too!* This was the cry of Israel in 1 Samuel 8 and they got the one they deserved, *Saul*. God had warned them, but did they listen? He told them that this King was going to take away their sons to fight dangerous wars, their daughters to be cooks and bakers and would also take a proportion of their land, crops, slaves and flocks for his own use. *No, we want a King!* "Then don't come running back to me when it all goes wrong!" adds God, in 1 Samuel 8:18. "We don't care – give us a King, already!"

Samuel shows his credentials as a prophet by giving Saul the following instructions after anointing him; *you'll meet two men and this is what they will say . . . then you'll find another three men, this is what they'll be carrying and this is what they will do . . . then you will meet a company of prophets and you will prophesy with them!*

That's the sort of thing that a real prophet does!

So Saul becomes king. This first king of Israel was volatile, insecure and paranoid, which was probably God's punishment on Israel for showing such a lack of faith in Him and demanding a King in the first place.

The people wanted a King for a very good reason. It's the same reason why human beings throughout history have tried to do things their own way and have followed their human instincts in building their own empires and kingdoms. It's because we are wilful beings and, when push comes to shove, quite faithless. We still find it hard to trust God, (or even believe in Him these days) and, rather than waiting on Him, we go ahead with our own plans expecting His blessing when we have spent all of our energy and return to Him with a pleading heart to put things right.

So it was with the Children of Israel when Saul led them against the Ammonites. They had more faith in a flesh and blood, mortal, flawed King than they had in the Lord God, Creator of the universe, who had delivered them from slavery in Egypt, sustained them in the desert and fought on their behalf as they began to conquer the land. The prophet Samuel reminded them exactly *who* was in charge, after reminding them of all that God had done for them from the days of Moses onwards:

> *"And when you saw that Nahash the king of the children of Ammon came against you, you said to me, No! But a king will reign over us, when the* Lord *your God was your king. Now therefore here is the king whom you have chosen, whom you have desired! And, behold, the* Lord *has set a king over you."*
> (1 Samuel 12:12–13)

And as a further reminder he called on the Lord to send thunder and rain and declare His majesty. *See that your wickedness is great, which you have done in the sight of the* Lord, *in asking a king for yourselves,* he added.

It's the old chestnut of faith versus works, putting ourselves and our labours before a complete and sincere trust in God.

And what a king. Oy! He was disloyal to his son (14:45), didn't listen to God (15:8,11), lied under oath (19:6), communed with witches (28:7), went back on promises (26:2) and, as a result, was not respected by his people (14:36,40).

Samuel gives it to him straight:

> *"And Samuel said, Has the* Lord *as great delight in burnt offerings and sacrifices as in obeying the voice of the* Lord? *Behold, to obey is better than sacrifice, to listen is better than the fat of rams. For rebellion is like the sin of witchcraft, and stubbornness is like idolatry and image worship. Because you have rejected the word of the* Lord, *He has also rejected you from being king."*
> (1 Samuel 15:22–23)

God looks on the inside, on what motivates us and, if He sees rebellion and wilfulness, then there's trouble ahead, *bigger trouble* if He has raised you up to positions of influence and responsibility. This principle is unchanged. There are a lot of Christian leaders running around hither and thither in their own little worlds, proclaiming much but, in actual fact, living in rebellion because they are not doing what God originally asked them to do. You reject Him . . . *and He rejects you!*

But my ministry is growing, supporters are giving financially! Yes, but, even after God rejected Saul, he still experienced successes in battles with the Philistines, before he finally had to *face the music*. God looks at the *whole* picture, it's not just about you and me, you know. But He gets you in the end! A day will come when you have to explain yourself to Him face to face, so be warned!

Samuel went looking for a new king to anoint. He was led to the sons of Jesse.

> "But the LORD said to Samuel, **Do not look at his countenance or at the height of his stature because I have refused him!** For the LORD does not see as man sees, for man looks at the outward appearance, but the LORD looks at the heart."
> (1 Samuel 16:7)

This doesn't change. Notice that God is shouting these words, as He chooses the lowly, unimportant *David* as heir to Saul. There's great hope for us short, untidy chaps. God isn't populating His kingdom with the cast of Hollyoaks or Baywatch! He's looking for those who truly want to walk *The Way of the Lord*, irrespective of age, outward appearance, social class or brain power!

So David was the heir apparent, but Saul was not happy with this arrangement, particularly as this young shepherd was the only Israelite with the faith to take on the giant Goliath, let alone defeat him. This following speech says it all:

"Then David said to the Philistine, You come to me with a sword, with a spear, and with a shield, but I come to you in the name of the LORD of Hosts, the God of the armies of Israel Whom you have defied. This day the LORD will deliver you into my hand, and I shall strike you and take your head from you and I will give the carcasses of the army of the Philistines this day to the fowls of the air and to the wild beasts of the earth, so all the earth will know that there is a God in Israel. And all this assembly will know that the LORD does not save with sword and spear, for the battle is the LORD's and He will give you into our hands."
(1 Samuel 17:45–47)

David had the same understanding that Moses and Joshua had. *The battle is the LORD's!* If only the rest had such faith!

Do we have such faith in the very different battles that we fight?

The Second Book of Samuel

Curious name for a book, as Samuel is long gone by now, so he certainly didn't write it! To be honest, it hardly matters, as we all know the Author of this and every other book of the Bible. And did you know that this Author was the originator of the phrase, *how the mighty are fallen?*

This was David's remark at the demise of King Saul. This wasn't an exultation or boast, in fact there was a certain sadness about it:

"The beauty of Israel is slain upon your high places. How the mighty are fallen! Tell it not in Gath, publish it not in the streets of Ashkelon, lest the daughters of the Philistines rejoice, lest the daughters of the uncircumcised triumph."
(2 Samuel 1:19–20)

Saul may have been down, but his family were not yet down and out. Abner, Saul's army captain, had installed Saul's son as king over Israel, while David's original area of influence was in Judah, centred at Hebron. *Israel and Judah* – the northern Kingdom and the Southern Kingdom – cracks in the foundations had already begun to appear, well before the time they would eventually tear apart from each other many years later!

"Now there was a long war between the house of Saul and the house of David, but David grew stronger and stronger, and the house of Saul grew weaker and weaker."
(2 Samuel 3:1)

Isn't it amazing that some just can't see where the wind is blowing, in terms of God's plans and desires? For hadn't the prophet Samuel anointed David as Saul's successor earlier, something that surely all Israelites would have known? So why did the "northerners" still hold on to the old regime? Perhaps that is a feature of our human nature, clinging to the old, resistant to the new. It was certainly the case when Jesus appeared on the scene. *What about now?*

But, eventually, the inevitable happened and David was fully accepted.

"So all the elders of Israel came to the king to Hebron and king David made a covenant with them in Hebron before the LORD, and they anointed David king over Israel."
(2 Samuel 5:3)

David was to reign seven and a half years in Hebron and another thirty three years in Jerusalem (once he had conquered the city), as king over the northern and southern Kingdoms.

One of the first things he did was to organise the moving of the Ark of the Covenant from the house of Abinadab in Gibeah (not sure why it was kept in a house in the first place, even though his son was authorised to look after it?), to Jerusalem. There's the curious and much-commented-on episode of how

Uzzah, another son of Abinadab, stretched his hand to steady the cart carrying the Ark and touched the holy object.

> *"And the anger of the LORD was kindled against Uzzah, and God struck him there for his error. And there he died by the Ark of God."*
> (2 Samuel 6:7)

It seems a bit unfair, after all the chap was only trying to help, wasn't he? Maybe, but, as someone who had lived possibly his whole life in a house shared with the Ark of the Covenant, perhaps there was a hint of *over-familiarity* with an object so holy and sacred that it says in Numbers 4:15:

> *". . . but they will not touch any holy thing, lest they die . . ."*

Let's not forget that if God sets rules and boundaries, it's not up to us to ignore them, otherwise we must accept the consequences.

Eventually the Ark reached Jerusalem and David was full of joy at this, so much so that he:

> *"Danced before the LORD with all his might, and David was girded with a linen ephod."*
> (2 Samuel 6:14)

I was curious about this *ephod* and discovered that this is a garment worn by a priest, wherein was stored the Urim and Thummim, the objects mentioned earlier used to discern God's Will. Yet here we have David wearing the same. So, when we read, as we do many times, of David *inquiring of the LORD*, can we assume that he is using these objects to get God's directions on certain matters? Here's an example:

> *"And David inquired of the LORD saying, Will I go up to the Philistines? Will You deliver them into my hand? And the LORD said to*

David, Go up for I shall doubtless deliver the Philistines into your hand".

(2 Samuel 5:19)

So, maybe, unlike Moses and Abraham, David, for all his great standing in the "pantheon" of biblical heroes, *did not speak face to face* with God (or the Angel of the LORD). Interesting.

But God was certainly on his side and provided all of his victories in battle. *And the LORD helped David wherever he went.* (2 Samuel 8:6). But God was *definitely not* on his side when he committed adultery with Bathsheba and did the following to her poor husband, in a letter to his battle commander:

"Set Uriah in the forefront of the hottest battle and retire from him, so he will be smitten and die."

(2 Samuel 11:15)

Interestingly, he was repeating what Saul originally tried to do to him!

"And Saul said, Thus will you say to David, The king does not desire any bride-price, but a hundred foreskins of the Philistines to be avenged of the king's enemies. But Saul thought to make David fall by the hand of the Philistines."

(1 Samuel 18:25)

This was a major lapse of judgement and God had to send the prophet Nathan to David to confront him on this:

"Thus says the LORD God of Israel, I AM has anointed you king over Israel and I AM has delivered you out of the hand of Saul, and I gave you your master's house and your master's wives into your bosom and gave you the Houses of Israel and of Judah. And if that had been too little, I would moreover have given to you such and such things. Why have you despised the commandment of the LORD, to do that which is bad in His sight? You

*have killed Uriah the Hittite with the sword and have taken his wife
to be your wife and have slain him with the sword of the children of
Ammon."*
(2 Samuel 12:7–9)

David was punished, but, as a mark of the man, was truly
contrite and forgiven by God, who knew his heart and therefore
knew that this was a *true repentance*.

Here was a king who had to battle with an errant son,
Absalom, who tried to usurp his father and was eventually
killed because, *he was not God's man*. David also had continuing
skirmishes with men still loyal to Saul, such as *Shimei*, who
cursed David with these words:

"Come out. Come out! You bloody man, and you wicked man, the LORD
*has returned upon you all the blood of the house of Saul, in whose place
you have reigned, and the* LORD *has delivered the kingdom into the hand
of Absalom your son and, behold, you are taken in your bad behavior,
because you are a bloody man."*
(2 Samuel 16:7–8)

David had the humility to accept this outburst and even
accept that perhaps he deserved it and that it was prompted by
God Himself. Here was a King who took his God seriously!

We also start to see more cracks appearing between the
Northern and Southern Kingdoms, an ominous portent for
the future:

*"And there happened to be a wicked man there whose name was Sheba,
the son of Bichri, a Benjamite, and he blew the shofar and said, We have
no part in David, neither do we have inheritance in the son of Jesse. Every
man to his tents, O Israel. So every man of Israel went up from after
David and followed Sheba the son of Bichri, but the men of Judah clung
to their king, from the Jordan even to Jerusalem."*
(2 Samuel 20:1–2)

Needless to say that Sheba was dealt with by David's military commander, Joab and order was resumed.

The story of David approaches its end, but not before one last major lapse of judgement, perhaps to show us the humanity of the man. Against the better judgement of his advisor, David decided to take a census of his people. This was not a good idea. Why not? Well, for a start, it seems that the idea was Satan's and that ain't a good start!

> *"And Satan stood up against Israel and provoked David to number Israel."*
> (1 Chronicles 21:1)

But Greek minds would dispute this and scream "inconsistency"! This is because of the following verse:

> *"And again the anger of the LORD was kindled against Israel, and He moved David against them to say, Go, number Israel and Judah."*
> (2 Samuel 24:1)

This "discrepancy" is one of those often quoted by those wishing to discredit the Bible. *Who told David to make a census, God or Satan?* The key to this is simply to use your common sense knowing that Satan is *always* going to want to provoke God and that God sometimes *allows* Satan leeway in order to provide a lesson to mankind (e.g. in the story of Job). So it's simply a case of Satan moving David to take the census and God allowing this out of righteous anger. And the reason why taking a census was a particularly bad thing anyway was that Israel did not belong to David and so he had no right to do so.

When this was completed nine months later, David realised that this was not a good thing and he pleaded with God to forgive him. It wasn't as easy as that. Through the prophet, *Gad*, he was given three choices of punishment. Either seven years of famine, or three months of fleeing from his enemies, or three days of pestilence in the land.

> *"And David said to Gad, I am in a great strait. Let us now fall into the hand of the* Lord, *for His mercies are great. And* **Do not let me fall into the hand of man!"**
> (2 Samuel 24:14)

He had accepted the third option, resulting in the death of 70,000 men. It seems a harsh decision by him and by God and the death toll would have been more if David hadn't intervened. He was instructed to build an altar in the threshing floor of Araunah the Jebusite and made burnt offerings and peace offerings.

The plague was halted. These were certainly different times to ours. Or perhaps not, perhaps we have just lost sight of God and His ways? Perhaps we've been angering God? How would we know? A frightening thought.

From Israel to exile

The First Book of Kings

The story of King Solomon has a fissure running right through it. In just a few short verses he goes from mega-hero to super-dud, shuffling out of the story with a premature death and one of the worst legacies of any Bible character. How did it get to this?

It starts off well enough, with a handover from his father, King David.

> *"I am going the way of all the earth. Be strong therefore, and show yourself to be a man, and keep the charge of the LORD your God, to walk in His ways, to keep His statutes, His commandments, His judgments, and His testimonies, as it is written in the Torah (Teaching) of Moses, so you will have insight in all that you do and wherever you turn yourself."*
> (1 Kings 2:2–3)

David also expected his son to settle a few scores, with the admonition to *let not his hoary head go down to the grave in peace* (for Joab) and *you will bring down his hoary head to the grave with blood* (for Shimei)

As a King you would expect Solomon to have been David's heir apparent, his first-born. In fact he was at least the tenth official son, not including a collection of *unofficial* sons, born from his mistresses. So you would expect other sons to be a bit miffed by this. We read of *Absolom*, David's third son, a bit earlier. We now read of his fourth son, *Adonijah*, who made a bid for the throne, but was killed for his efforts, at Solomon's command. Solomon knew that he alone was *God's man* and nothing was allowed to get in the way of this destiny.

God told him as much in this first encounter, as a teenager:

> *"In Gibeon the LORD appeared to Solomon in a dream by night and God said, Ask what I shall give you."*
> (1 Kings 3:5)

He asked for an understanding heart to be able to be a good judge of his people. He got this and more. He got riches and honour and even the promise of a long life.

Yet he died young, in his fifties. Where did it all go wrong? Well, his reign starts off well, with peace reigning throughout the land and Solomon gaining great riches and an international reputation as a man of great wisdom, as well as the author of 3,000 proverbs and 1,005 songs. Considering past days, there's a strange atmosphere of bonhomie in Judah and Israel.

> *"Judah and Israel were many as the sand which is by the sea in multitude, eating and drinking, and making merry."*
> (1 Kings 4:20)

The great Jerusalem temple was constructed, involving tens of thousands of labourers and workmen, taking seven years to complete. But, tellingly, his *own palace* took thirteen years to complete. Is this significant?

When the Ark of the Covenant is then moved from David's City to the newly built Temple and *God's Glory Cloud fills the House of the LORD*, you get the sense that the honeymoon period is over. God (through Solomon himself) reminds His people, that He is very much involved in their lives, in the way that they live, in their successes on the battle field, in the functions of plagues and famines, in the way they deal with their neighbours. This was followed by a major sacrifice of 22,000 oxen and 120,000 sheep and a fourteen day feast throughout the land.

Then a warning! God appears a second time to Solomon. He reads the riot act, the promises of blessings (if Solomon follows the Torah) and curses (if he didn't). Why was this needed? Wasn't Solomon the *wisest man who ever lived*? He knew what side of his bread was buttered!

But God knew . . . Solomon's major weakness, which was to bring a very swift downfall. *His love for the ladies.*

His first wife was Pharaoh's daughter, a strategic coupling but seemingly a successful one. But then, at our *fissure point*, Chapter 11, we see something new.

> *"But king Solomon loved many foreign women together with the daughter of Pharaoh, women of the Moabites, Ammonites, Edomites, Sidonians, Hittites, of the nations which the LORD said to the children of Israel, You will not go in to them, neither will they come in to you, for surely they will turn away your heart after their gods: Solomon clung to these in love. And he had seven hundred wives, princesses, and three hundred concubines: and his wives turned away his heart."*
>
> (1 Kings 11:1–3)

How stupid was he? And I repeat the words from an earlier Chapter, *didn't He know with Whom he was dealing?* Let's see the results of these dalliances:

> *"For Solomon went after Ashtoret the goddess of the Sidonians, and after Milkom the abomination of the Ammonites. And Solomon did bad things in the sight of the LORD, and did not go fully after the LORD, as had David his father. Then Solomon built a high place for Chemosh, the abomination of Moab on the hill that is before Jerusalem and for Molekh, the abomination of the children of Ammon. And he did likewise for all his foreign wives, who burned incense and sacrificed to their gods."*
>
> (1 Kings 11:5–8)

And the immediate, inevitable consequence?

> *"And the* LORD *was angry with Solomon, because his heart was turned from the* LORD *God of Israel, Who had appeared to him twice and had commanded him concerning this thing, that he should not go after other gods, but he did not keep that which the* LORD *commanded."*
> (2 Kings 11:9–10)

This was followed immediately by the awful legacy mentioned at the head of the chapter:

> *"Therefore the* LORD *said to Solomon, Since you have done this and you have not kept My covenant and My statutes, which I have commanded you, I shall surely tear the kingdom from you and will give it to your servant. Only in your days I shall not do it for David your father's sake, I shall tear it out of the hand of your son. However, I shall not tear away the whole kingdom, but will give one tribe to your son for David My servant's sake, and for the sake of Jerusalem which I have chosen."*
> (1 Kings 11:11–13)

Solomon, through his lustful ways and complete disregard for the God who had given him so much (perhaps *too much* by our reckoning?), had sealed the fate of his people for years and years and brought about *the final separation* of Israel (the northern kingdom) and Judah (the southern kingdom).

God set to work immediately to carry out this judgement, stirring up other nations against Solomon. It seems a constant theme during those times that, although the lens of history is focused on the free-will activities of the leaders and Kings of Israel, the other nations seem to have *less free-will* and are *hardened* or *stirred up* in order to carry out God's purposes for His chosen people. This theme will re-appear again, so keep your eyes peeled!

One wonders if this is still true today as God never changes, just our perception of Him. God does not change, it is just we who have moved on . . . and forgotten His ways.

One such irritant was *Jeroboam*, the son of a servant, who God raised up as a direct internal threat to Solomon. He became the King of Israel, the northern kingdom, which then split from Judah. In the meantime, Solomon dies (God has no more use for him) and is replaced by his son, *Rehoboam*.

"And when Rehoboam came to Jerusalem, he assembled the entire House of Judah, with the tribe of Benjamin, a hundred eighty thousand chosen men who were warriors, to fight against the House of Israel, to bring the kingdom back to Rehoboam the son of Solomon."
(1 Kings 12:21)

A prophet, *Shemaiah*, was needed to speak sense to Rehoboam.

"Thus says the LORD, You will not go up or fight against your brothers the children of Israel. Each man return to his house, for this thing is from Me. Therefore they listened to the word of the LORD and turned and went away, according to the word of the LORD."
(1 Kings 12:24)

At least someone was listening to God.

What follows is a record of (mostly) misdemeanours of various Kings of Israel and Judah, with the odd good King of Judah, for instance Asa and Jehosophat, providing some welcome relief to sordid tales of idol worship and general *anarchy*. The Hebrew word that is used to express this is *Ra*, often translated as "bad, evil or wicked" but is best expressed as the *opposite* of *Shalom*, in the sense of uneasiness or chaos and the fact that nothing seems to fit. It is perhaps a fair description of life today, with its uncertainties and uneasiness and our sense that people's lives are not as free as they once were in less complicated times.

Those were dark days indeed, particularly in the Kingdom of Israel. One of the worst of a bad bunch was King Ahab:

"And Ahab the son of Omri brought anarchy in the sight of the LORD above all who were before him. And it was as if it had been a light thing for him to walk in the sins of Jeroboam the son of Nebat, that he took to wife Jezebel the daughter of Etbaal king of the Sidonians, and went and served Baal and worshipped him. And he raised an altar for Baal in the house of Baal that he had built in Samaria. Ahab made an Asherah and Ahab did more to provoke the LORD God of Israel to anger than all the kings of Israel who were before him."
(1 Kings 16:30–33)

God raised up the prophet *Elijah* as an irritant for this awful King, the man who met God as a *still small voice* and who was part of a remnant numbering just seven thousand who had remained true to their God.

In a final confrontation with Ahab, Elijah makes this fierce proclamation:

"Because you have sold yourself to work an awful thing in the sight of the LORD, behold, I shall bring evil upon you and will take away your posterity and will cut off from Ahab every male, and him that is shut up and left in Israel. And will make your house like the house of Jeroboam the son of Nebat, and like the house of Basha the son of Ahijah, for the provocation with which you have provoked Me to anger and made Israel to sin. And the LORD also spoke of Jezebel saying, The dogs will eat Jezebel by the wall of Jezreel. He of Ahab who dies in the city the dogs will eat, and he who dies in the field the fowls of the air will eat. But there was no one like Ahab, who sold himself to work wickedness in the sight of the LORD, whom Jezebel his wife stirred up. And he did very abominably in following idols, according to all things that the Amorite did, whom the LORD cast out before the children of Israel."
(1 Kings 21:20–26)

If you are sick of hearing how the "Old Testament" is all about laws and regulations and that grace doesn't appear until "New Testament" times, then read on.

"And it was, when Ahab heard those words that he tore his clothes and put sackcloth on his flesh, and fasted, and lay in sackcloth, and went softly."
(1 Kings 21:27)

And what does God do? This man, who was the very worst of a bad bunch, was *granted leniency* because of his repentance.

"And the word of the LORD came to Elijah the Tishbite saying, Do you see how Ahab humbles himself before Me? Because he humbles himself before Me, I shall not bring the evil in his days, but I shall bring the evil upon his house in his son's days."
(1 Kings 21:28–29)

We serve a remarkable God. How very unlike us He is!

The Second Book of Kings

The opening few verses are not a good start. The King of Israel fell down a hole and asked Baal whether he was going to recover. Instead, the *true God* of Israel tells him, through Elijah the prophet, that he's *going to die*. Even worse, he's going to die *because* he went to the wrong god! That's how far Israel had veered away from God's yardstick in those days.

Elijah was soon taken from this world, in a whirlwind accompanied by chariot of fires and his prophetic mantle (possibly a prayer shawl) was given to young Elisha, his protégé, who asked for a *double portion* of Elijah's spirit. He certainly received this *and then some*, when one peruses the catalogue of miracles performed in his subsequent ministry, only surpassed by the later ministry of Jesus the Messiah!

During this period the land is served by a largely evil crew of Kings, with Israel generally suffering more than Judah on this score. In 841 BC King Jehu was the new King in Israel, ordered to finally rid the earth of the house of Ahab on account of the sins of Jezebel. Jezebel met her end thrown out of the palace window by a pair of eunuchs, so another royal dynasty disappeared and a new one was created. Would this one be any better? 2 Kings 10:18 appears to set the tone for this man's rule: "*Ahab served Baal a little; Jehu will serve him much*", he declared. But this was a clever deception to flush out the priests of Baal, who were done to death. Despite this Jehu didn't completely turn away from the dark side.

We can get a flavour of those times, by reading the account of King Jehoahaz of Israel:

"*In the twenty-third year of Joash the son of Ahaziah king of Judah, Jehoahaz the son of Jehu began to reign over Israel in Samaria, and reigned seventeen years. And he did that which was evil in the sight of the LORD and followed the sins of Jeroboam the son of Nebat, who made Israel to sin. He did not depart from it.*"
(2 Kings 13:1–2)

This is a standard formula particularly for the Kings of Israel. And there are usually consequences:

"*And the anger of the LORD was kindled against Israel and He delivered them into the hand of Hazael king of Syria, and into the hand of Ben-Hadad the son of Hazael, all their days.*"
(2 Kings 13:3)

But God was always open to a change of heart:

"*And Jehoahaz sought the LORD, and the LORD hearkened to him, for He saw the oppression of Israel, because the king of Syria oppressed them. And the LORD gave Israel a savior, so that they went out from under the hand of the Syrians. And the children of Israel lived in their tents as before.*"
(2 Kings 13:4–5)

We move ahead a few years and cast our eyes now to Judah, the Southern Kingdom, to yet another bad king, *Ahaz*, he who

*made his son to pass through the fire, according to the abominations
of the nations, whom the* LORD *cast out from before the children of
Israel* (2 Kings 16:3).

Unfortunately he was the King who crossed the line when,
to help him in fighting the Syrians, did a *deal with the devil* . . .
the Assyrians.

> *"So Ahaz sent messengers to Tiglat-Pileser king of Assyria saying, I am
> your servant and your son: come up and save me from the hand of the
> king of Syria and from the hand of the king of Israel, who is rising up
> against me."*
> (2 Kings 16:7)

To do this he took silver and gold from God's Temple.
Perhaps not the wisest move! Later on he even constructed a
pagan altar in the Temple and made offerings on it. How God
never smote him where he stood is a mystery. Instead we hear
of Ahaz living to a reasonable age, then "sleeping with his
fathers".

But what did happen soon after was that *Hoshea*, the King
of Israel at this time, also sucked up to the Assyrians. For his
troubles he was slung into prison and Israel was besieged for
three years, then conquered and the People of Israel led into
captivity. God's patience had run out. Retribution had been
long coming, as we read:

> *"For so it was that the children of Israel had sinned against the* LORD
> *their God, Who had brought them up out of the land of Egypt, from
> under the hand of Pharaoh king of Egypt and had revered other gods
> and walked in the statutes of the nations and of the kings of Israel,
> which they had made, whom the* LORD *cast out from before the children
> of Israel. And the children of Israel did secretly the things that were not
> right against the* LORD *their God and they built high places for themselves
> in all their cities, from the tower of the watchmen to the fortified city.
> And they set up pillars and groves for themselves on every high hill and*

under every green tree. And there they burned incense in all the high places, as did the nations whom the LORD carried away before them, and wrought wicked things to provoke the LORD to anger, and they served idols, of which the LORD had said to them, You will not do this thing."
(2 Kings 17:7–12)

The Northern Kingdom of Israel was no more and its people largely vanish into obscurity, kept alive by a multitude of myths about the 'Lost Tribes of Israel'. This is a pointless exercise, in the same vein as musing over the whereabouts of Atlantis or the pot of gold at the end of the rainbow. If God wants a people 'lost', then that's it, they're LOST. The Northern Kingdom simply went the way of the multitude of peoples, like the Canaanites, Philistines and Moabites, who served their purpose in His plans, but then disappear from the pages of history.

This is not to say that the ten tribes were *totally* lost, only those who were living in the Northern Kingdom at the time of the exile. Many had left earlier. Some remained in the Southern Kingdom when the kingdoms first split (1 Kings 12:17). Some returned there a few years after the split (2 Chronicles 11:14–17). Others returned at various points, appalled at the growing apostasy of the Northern Kingdom. You can read about these in 2 Chronicles 15:9 and 2 Chronicles 30:25–26. The point I wish to make is that, although Jews are said to have descended from the folk of the Southern Kingdom of Judah, it is safe to say that *all tribes* were represented among these people, not just Judah and Benjamin.

Rather than let the Northern Kingdom stay empty, the Assyrians populated it with people from the pagan lands to the north and the east. This was normal practice for them, but what they failed to realise was that this was a *far from normal* situation. This was God's land. He had said so in Leviticus 25:23:

"The land must not be sold permanently, because the land is mine and you are but aliens and my tenants."

To teach them this, God sent lions to terrorise them:

> *"So they spoke to the king of Assyria saying, The nations which you have removed and placed in the cities of Samaria do not know the manner of the God of the land, therefore He has sent lions among them and, behold, they are slaying them because they do not know the manner of the God of the land."*
> (2 Kings 17:26)

So a priest was brought back to teach them how to revere God, although it didn't stop them from worshipping their own pagan gods.

Meanwhile, the Southern Kingdom was blessed with a good King, *Hezekiah*. He removed the high places, shattered the idols and did his best to bring back the old ways. But he still feared the King of Assyria more than he feared God. He stripped the Temple of all of its silver and much of its gold and gave it to the pagan tyrant. As history is going to show us again and again, appeasement tends not to work. And this was no exception.

The Assyrians came and lay siege to Jerusalem. And, in their arrogance, they taunted the Judeans.

> *"Thus says the king, **Do not let Hezekiah deceive you!** For he will not be able to deliver you out of his hand. **Do not let Hezekiah make you trust in the Lord!** Saying, the Lord will surely deliver us, and this city will not be delivered into the hand of the king of Assyria. **Do not listen to Hezekiah!** . . ."*
> (2 Kings 18:29–31)

The Assyrian King had boasted that every other god had crumbled before him. Why should the God of Judah be any different? God was not impressed and assured His people that the King of Assyria would not take Jerusalem and reminded them *Who* would be fighting for them:

"For out of Jerusalem will go forth a remnant, and those who escape out of Mount Zion: the zeal of the LORD of Hosts will do this."
(2 Kings 19:31)

The LORD of Hosts, whom we met in 1 Samuel, leader of the mighty heavenly army, proved His power and *185,000 Assyrian soldiers were killed by the Angel of the LORD that very night.* And, as an epitaph:

"So Sennacherib king of Assyria departed and went and returned and lived at Nineveh. And it was, as he was worshipping in the house of Nisrokh his god, that Adramelekh and Sarezer his sons struck him with the sword and they escaped into the land of Ararat . . ."
(2 Kings 19:36–37)

How the mighty have fallen.

You see the pattern. God uses Assyria to carry out judgement against Israel, but when the Assyrians actually start to believe that they were masters of their own fate, He decimates their army and kills their King. This is a biblical principal in action, that our world should take great heed of. *God is in charge of the baddies as well as the goodies!*

You can't choose your family and Hezekiah's son, Manasseh, was probably the worst King of all.

"And he did that which was bad in the sight of the LORD, after the abominations of the nations, whom the LORD cast out before the children of Israel."
(2 Kings 21:2)

Manasseh was the *straw that broke the camel's back* and it is because of his many evil acts that God chose to hold back no longer:

"And the LORD spoke by His servants the prophets saying, Because Manasseh king of Judah has done these abominations, having done

wickedly above all that the Amorite did, who were before him, and has made Judah also to sin with his idols: therefore thus says the Lord God of Israel, Behold, I am bringing such evil upon Jerusalem and Judah, that whoever hears of it, both his ears will tingle."
(2 Kings 21:10–12)

But this doesn't happen during his reign. Ironically it starts to happen during the reign of his saintly grandson, *Josiah*, the righteous King who discovers the ancient scrolls of the Torah and dedicated his people to God, cleansing the land and the people.

"And there was no king before him like him, who turned to the Lord with all his heart, and with his entire being, and with all his might, according to all the Torah (Teaching) of Moses, nor did any like him rise after him."
(2 Kings 23:25)

But, in the very next verse:

"Nevertheless the Lord did not turn from the fierceness of His great wrath, by which His anger was kindled against Judah because of all the provocations with which Manasseh had provoked Him".
(2 Kings 23:26)

God brought judgement in the reign of Josiah's son.

"And the Lord sent against him bands of the Chaldeans, bands of the Syrians, bands of the Moabites, and bands of the children of Ammon and sent them against Judah to destroy it, according to the word of the Lord, which He spoke by His servants the prophets."
(2 Kings 24:2)

The Babylonians came, saw and conquered.

The Book of Jonah

During those troublesome times in Judah and Israel, God raised up many prophets to talk sense to them. Jonah was one such prophet, living in Israel during the time of Jereboam II.

> *"He restored the border of Israel from the entrance of Hamath to the sea of the plain, according to the word of the LORD God of Israel, which He spoke by the hand of his servant Jonah, the son of Amittai the prophet, who was from Gath Hepher."*
> (2 Kings 14:25)

Here was a prophet with a death wish. In this short book, he contemplated his own death on *three* occasions, for different reasons. The first time was out of *guilt*, that his disobedience to God's call was the cause of the storm that threatened the lives of all the men on his 'getaway' ship. This is the first clue that Jonah was no coward, but just a wilful man, preferring his own ways but resigned to his fate now that God had caught up with him.

Yet God still used this episode to draw others to Himself.

> *"So they took Jonah and cast him into the sea and the sea ceased from its raging. Then the men revered the LORD exceedingly and offered a sacrifice to the LORD and made vows."*
> (Jonah 1:15–16)

Isn't it marvellous that God can still use us in our weaknesses, despite ourselves?!

Then there's that fish thing. Did Jonah actually realise he was in the belly of a whale? The text seems to imply that he'd thought he'd drowned and was at the gates of the underworld ("the earth with her bars" Jonah 2:7). So perhaps he did die, then.

The second time Jonah contemplated his death was out of *shame*. Jonah did his early runner because he felt, in a pique of self-righteousness, that the wicked people of Nineveh *did not deserve salvation*. Now that he's decided to do what God asked, and preach to them, he is *dismayed* (even angry) at the results of his preaching! And he's not happy with himself.

> *"Therefore now, LORD, take, I beseech You, my life from me, for it is better for me to die than to live."*
> (Jonah 4:3)

Let's face it, we can spend a lifetime fruitlessly preaching at kindly Uncle Arthur to find peace with God before it's too late, but that incorrigible cad, Bruce, repented and accepted Christ at the first hearing. *It's so unfair according to our Jonah inclination, isn't it?* The fact is that none of us *deserve* salvation. God saves whom He saves, even some unsavoury characters *who definitely don't deserve it* (in our humble opinion)! That, for me, is the legacy of Jonah, *not* the person in the ship who's dooming us to a watery grave.

The final death-wish seems to be because he was a bit of a wimp who preferred his comforts, but mainly that he was unhappy living in a world where a useful plant could just live for a single day before suffering a death by worm. God used this as an example to show Jonah the value of human life, that surely 120,000 of them (plus animals) were worth more tears than the life of a single plant.

Did Jonah learn his lesson? We are never told. The real point is, have *we* learned the lesson? Do we yearn for the salvation of the unlovely, the rogues, the *undeserving*? Do we really?

The Book of Joel

This prophet lived at around the same time, perhaps a bit earlier. The trouble is that there are no clues in the text as to background, except to say that he was the son of Pethuel and that the context places him in the Southern Kingdom of Judah.

There are no clues because the whole book is just a single prophecy. It's been much quoted (and misquoted) and many modern teachers apparently 'want a piece of it', claiming it for their own purposes. Here's an example (taken from my book, *How the Church Lost the Way*):

A certain TV preacher spoke of the Feast of Tabernacles, *Sukkot*. The crux of his argument was linking Joel Chapter 2 with the festival. But nowhere in Hebrew Scripture or Jewish Tradition do the verses in Joel Chapter 2 have any relevance to Sukkot.

The passage he dwelt on was Joel 2:18–27. In its context the passage has Joel promising the people of Israel that God would restore things to them if they repent. It was not too late for them. Now this has nothing to do with the theme or the setting of Sukkot. He took one small part of it.

> *"Be glad then, ye children of Zion, and rejoice in the* LORD *your God: for he hath given you the former rain moderately, and he will cause to come down for you the rain, the former rain, and the latter rain in the first month."*
> (Joel 2:23, KJV)

He took the phrase "in the first month" and assumed that this was referring to the month of Tishrei, the autumn month of the Jewish *civil* New Year, the month of Sukkot, the Feast of Tabernacles.

There's a big problem with this. Never in the Bible is the first month *anything other* than Nisan, in spring, the time of Passover. So we could actually stop here because we have taken away the whole foundation of his argument – his tenuous and faulty link between Joel Chapter 2 and the Feast of Tabernacles. But it actually gets worse. Here is verse 19:

> *"Yea, the* LORD *will answer and say unto his people, Behold, I will send you corn, and wine, and oil, and ye shall be satisfied therewith: and I will no more make you a reproach among the heathen:"*
> (KJV – the version he was using)

Here is the TV preacher's take on the first part of this verse: *Yea, the* LORD *will answer and say unto his people, Behold, I will send you money, and blessing, and anointing (so no weapon may prosper against you).*

So, according to him, these are the rewards you will receive. And how will you receive them? Another scripture twist, in verse 23.

"*Be glad then, ye children of Zion, and rejoice in the* LORD *your God . . .*"

(KJV)

His take on *rejoicing* is for you to send money to the ministry that he was working for. Rejoicing implies action and God clearly intended this to be your reaching for your wallet. Only by doing so will you unlock these financial blessings, which will also include a *double portion* (how he arrived at that remains totally unexplained) for you.

So what have we learned from this? How can we guard against these misuses? Well, one sign to take heed of is when someone tells you that God *has spoken prophetically* to him, using Scripture. *God spoke to me prophetically* . . . Oh dear. Much discernment needed here.

Joel provides much material for such people. Another widely (mis-)used theme is that of the army of locusts in the book. Who are they? How are they to be interpreted? Before we consider this, let's examine the whole book.

It reads like the end chapters of Deuteronomy, blessings and curses and their consequences, except here they are more concise, direct and urgent.

"*For a nation has come upon My land, strong and without number, whose teeth are the teeth of a lion and he has the cheek teeth of a great lion.*"

(Joel 1:6)

Sounds like the Assyrians, though you never know with prophecy. We need to read more.

He's suggesting that the people should act, and act swiftly, led by the priests:

> *"Woe for the Day! For the Day of the* Lord *is at hand and it will come as a destruction from the Almighty."*
> (Joel 1:15)

The urgency is then moved up a notch:

> *"Blow the shofar in Zion! Sound an alarm on My holy mountain! Let all the inhabitants of the land tremble, for the Day of the* Lord *has come, for it is near at hand; a Day of darkness and of gloominess, a Day of clouds and of thick darkness, as the morning spreads over the mountains, a great and strong people. There has never been the like, neither will there be any more after it, to the years of many generations."*
> (Joel 2:1–2)

We now move into apocalyptic scenarios, alluding to a terrible day like no other. There's every reason to believe that this day has not yet fully come. The marauding locusts are then described:

> *"Their appearance is like the appearance of horses, and as horsemen, so will they run. They will leap on the tops of mountains like the noise of chariots, like the noise of a flame of fire that devours the stubble, as a strong people set in battle array."*
> (Joel 2:4–5)

So is this a mighty end-time army of Christians, as some believe? If they choose to believe so, then so be it. The verses tend to say otherwise but sometimes, the way we interpret Scripture is determined by what flavour of theology we subscribe to. If, for instance, you are a *postmillennialist*, believing that the

Church will triumph over the world, then the thought of an end-time army may be appealing to you. But is it Bible truth?

A few verses later are very reminiscent of the stark scenarios painted in the Book of Revelation:

> *"The earth will quake before them, the heavens will tremble. The sun and the moon will be dark, and the stars will withdraw their shining. And the LORD will utter His voice before His army for His camp is very great, for He Who executes His word is strong, for the Day of the LORD is great and very terrible and who can abide it?"*
> (Joel 2:10–11)

Again, the Day of the LORD. We will meet this again later.

There's a call to repentance and a call for restoration, followed by a list of seven blessings, beloved by the prosperity preachers, who tear them screaming out of context and gorge on them. You, discerning reader, are urged to read them for yourselves, in context, in Joel 2:23–27, noticing that they are directed primarily to the *children of Zion*.

Then the famous passage, read so often as a liturgy of hope at charismatic assemblies. The verses repeated by Simon in the Temple, after the Holy Spirit has poured down on those pilgrims at the Feast of *Shavuot* (Pentecost).

> *"And it will be afterward that I shall pour out My Spirit upon all flesh and your sons and your daughters will prophesy, your old men will dream dreams, your young men will see visions, and I shall pour out My Spirit also upon the servants and upon the hand maidens in those days, and I shall show wonders in the heavens and in the earth, blood and fire and pillars of smoke. The sun will be turned into darkness and the moon into blood, before the great and the terrible Day of the LORD comes."*
> (Joel 3:2–4 – this is Joel 2:28–31 in other versions)

How tempting it is to cherry-pick and just claim the first two verses for ourselves, yet ignore the other events that seem intertwined with them, the talk of blood, fire and heavenly signs. If we are not yet in the time-frame of the Day of the LORD, then perhaps our sons, daughters, old men and young men have *not yet* been empowered in the ways suggested.

The logic of it and the gut feeling suggest that the fullness of this prophecy really is *still to come* as are the events in Chapter 4, the gathering of the Nations in the Valley of Jehoshaphat. Here's a taster:

> *"For, behold, in those days, and in that time, when I shall bring back the captivity of Judah and Jerusalem, I shall also gather all the nations and will bring them down into the Valley of Jehoshaphat, and will plead with them there for My people and for My heritage Israel, whom they have scattered among the nations, and parted My land."*
>
> (Joel 4:1–2 – this is Joel 3:1–2 in other versions)

Too awe-inspiring to contemplate, but nevertheless in the Word of God. It will be a time when the relativism and uncertainty of our age are swept away by events and we will have to decide whose side we will be on, God's side or *not* on God's side. Surely our time in eternity will depend on this decision.

CHAPTER

6

We told you so!

The Book of Amos

This prophet was a contemporary of Jonah, living in the Northern Kingdom at the time of King Jeroboam II. His book is one complete prophecy directed at a number of targets, with a short interlude in Chapter seven when Jeroboam's priest tried to ban him for daring to speak against one of them, the King himself.

It is useful, when looking at the minor prophets, to brandish a one or two-word description that sums up their whole book. I would suggest Jonah would be *rebellion* (rather than "bringer of bad luck") and Joel would be *judgement*. What about Amos? Well, the usual word bandied about is *justice*. There's a ministry called *The Amos Trust* that, despite providing no source texts for its name from the Bible, suggests that it "promotes justice and hope for forgotten communities." Where does this idea come from? Is it a good summary of the book? Let us see.

He starts off castigating the pagan nations and cities for their aggressive and war-like behaviour. But then he turns to God's people, first Judah, rebuking them for neglecting the Torah. But his main target is *Israel*, the Northern Kingdom, who are well and truly *laid into*.

First he reminds them what God has done for them, destroying their enemies and rescuing them from Egyptian slavery. Then in a brilliantly poetic passage at the start of Chapter 3, he reminds them that the prophets are to be taken seriously and then he prophesies:

"Listen! Obey this word! You heifers of Bashan, in the mountain of Samaria who oppress the poor, crush the needy, who say to their masters, Bring and let us drink. Adonai, the Lord, has sworn by His holiness that, lo, the days will come upon you that He will take you away with hooks and your posterity with fish hooks. And you will go out through the breaches, each one through that which is before her, and you will cast yourselves into Harmon, says the Lord."
(Amos 4:1–3)

Then with delicious sarcasm he encourages them to continue worshipping at the pagan altars and to continue to *ignore* all of the warning signs that God has given them, the droughts, famines, blights, pestilences and defeats. How can a people have grown so dull, so insensitive, so unaware of the divine cord that connected them to unseen realities? You'd think they were mainstream Christians living in 21st Century Britain! More of that later.

Yet He gives them a chance first, perhaps this is the *last-chance saloon?*

"For thus says the Lord to the House of Israel, Seek Me and you will live."
(Amos 5:4)

He gives His credentials, to remind them Who they are dealing with:

"He Who made the seven stars, Pleiades and Orion, turns the shadow of death into the morning, makes the day dark with night, Who calls for the waters of the sea, and pours them out over the face of the earth, the Lord is His name, Who causes destruction to break out on the strong, so that destruction will come against the fortress."
(Amos 5:8–9)

Well, that's the *divine* calling card, so what about theirs? He then reminds them of their injustices against the poor and the pleadings of the prophets and warns them that the tables are about to be turned and they are about to be shocked out of their complacency:

". . . You have built houses of hewn stone, but you will not live in them. You have planted pleasant vineyards, but you will not drink wine from them."
(Amos 5:11)

And then, a motif, that is going to repeat *again and again* in Scripture and holds fast as much in our days as it did then:

"I hate, I despise your feast days and I shall not smell the burning sacrifices in your solemn assemblies. Though you offer Me burnt offerings and your meal offering, I shall not accept them. Nor will I even glance at the peace offerings of your fat beasts."
(Amos 5: 21–22)

It's the heart, the motivations, the inner life that interests God, not our outward *acts of piety.*

He even hated their melodies and songs, instead, *let justice run down like waters and acts of loving kindness like a mighty stream* (Amos 5:24).

He then hits them with His judgement, *Therefore I shall cause you to go into captivity beyond Damascus, says the* Lord, *Whose name is God of Hosts* (Amos 5:27).

There then follows a lengthy diatribe against Israel:

". . . Then the Lord *said to me, The end has come upon My people Israel. I shall not again pass by them any more. And the songs of the Temple will be howlings in that Day: the word of Adonai the* Lord. *There will be many dead bodies in every place, they will cast them out with silence . . . And I shall turn your feasts into mourning and all your songs into lamentation and I shall bring up sackcloth upon all loins and baldness*

upon every head and I shall make it like the mourning for an only son, and its end as a bitter day."
(Amos 8:2–3, 10)

There will even be a sign in the sky to show His displeasure:

*"And it will be in that Day, says Adonai, the L*ORD*, that I shall cause the sun to go down at noon and I will darken the earth on the clear day."*
(Amos 8:9)

This is a matter of historical record. It was the solar eclipse of June 15th, 763 BC, known as the Assyrian eclipse, as it was mentioned in their records too.

God had had enough with Israel and more judgement is promised, with the inevitable conclusion:

"For, behold, I AM *commanding and I shall sift the House of Israel among all the nations, like grain is sifted in a sieve, yet the least grain will not fall upon the earth."*
(Amos 9:9)

But, a promise is given, of restoration, just as we had at the end of the Book of Joel. But it's not a restoration of the House of Israel, rather it is the House of David, *Judah* (and a remnant from Israel), who will return to the land at a later unspecified date:

*"On that Day I shall raise up the Booth of David that has fallen and close up its breaches, and I shall raise up its ruins and I shall build it as in the days of old so they can possess the remnant of Edom and of all the nations that are called by My name, says the L*ORD *Who does this."*
(Amos 9:11–12)

If we are to summarise this book, although *justice* is the unique motif of Amos, it is just a symptom of the general malaise brought about by the Northern Kingdom's complete neglect of the One True God.

The Book of Hosea

Yet another prophet, alongside Jonah and Amos, living in the Northern Kingdom at the time of Jeroboam II. Hosea is the prophet who really had to *take one for the team*! He had to marry a prostitute, as a living picture of the state of Israel at that time, *for the land has committed great harlotry, departing from the LORD*. (Hosea 1:2). It went further, with their first three offspring being given prophetic names; *Jezreel* (scattered), *Lo Ruhamah* (no compassion) and *Lo Ami* (not my people). Bet they had a tough time in the schoolyard!

We then read of the points of similarities between the people of Israel and the activities of a harlot. The adulteries, the shameful lewd behaviour. This is explained well in this verse:

> *"And I shall visit upon her the days of the baalim, when she burned incense to them and she decked herself with her earrings and her jewels and she went after her lovers and forgot Me, says the LORD."*
> (Hosea 2:15 – this is Hosea 2:13 in other versions)

We are then given a glimpse of the future, perhaps as a reassurance from God that all is not completely lost for all time:

> *"And I shall betroth you to Me forever. Yes, I shall betroth you to Me in righteousness and in judgment and in loving kindness and in compassion."*
> (Hosea 2:21 – this is Hosea 2:19 in other versions)

Then Hosea is asked to rededicate himself to his unfaithful wife, asking her to change her ways. What we read here seems to be a prophecy of the *Galut*, the dispersion of the Jews throughout the world, followed by a wonderful restoration.

But then he returns to the condemnation of the current generation of Israel, for their neglect of God and His word, the Torah:

> *"My people are cut off, destroyed, for lack of knowledge. Because you have rejected knowledge, I will also reject you, so you will not be a priest to Me. Seeing you have forgotten the Torah (Teaching) of your God, I shall also forget your children."*
> (Hosea 4:6)

Harlotry is the major theme, *unfaithfulness*. That is the undeniable message of the book.

> *"I AM knows Ephraim, and Israel is not hidden from Me. For now, O Ephraim, you commit harlotry, Israel is defiled. They will not frame their doings to turn to their God, for the spirit of harlotry is in their midst and they have not known the LORD. And the pride of Israel testifies to His face, therefore Israel and Ephraim will fall in their iniquity, Judah also will fall with them. They will go with their flocks and with their herds to seek the LORD, but they will not find Him. He has withdrawn Himself from them."*
> (Hosea 5:3–6)

You may wonder why *Ephraim* is mentioned here, as well as Israel. In fact Ephraim is mentioned a lot in Hosea. The name also appears a lot in the literature of those who follow various theories regarding the "Lost Tribes of Israel" (including the Mormons). So what's the story?

Actually it's simple, but I'm going to use an unfamiliar word to describe it. Ephraim is used as a *synecdoche* to refer to the whole Northern Kingdom of Israel. A synecdoche is a term used when *a part of something* refers to the whole of something. A good example is when *London* is used instead of "British government", in the sense of "the political view from London is . . .". As the tribe of Ephraim is in the Northern Kingdom of Israel (and in fact King Jeroboam is of the tribe of Ephraim), then it is sometimes used *instead of* Israel. In fact, when the Northern Kingdom falls off the map, the name *Israel* is often used instead of Judah, just to complicate matters!

Here's a short passage that describes the situation very well:

"O Ephraim, what will I do to you? O Judah, what will I do to you? For your goodness is like a morning cloud and as the early dew it goes away. Therefore I have hewn them by the prophets. I have slain them by the words of My mouth and your judgments are like the light that goes forth. For I desire loving kindness and not sacrifice, and the knowledge of God more than burnt offerings."
(Hosea 6:4–6)

Then there's an ominous warning, one that could very much constitute one of the great themes in the Hebrew Scriptures:

"For they have sown the wind and they will reap the whirlwind . . ."
(Hosea 8:7)

This is a New Testament theme too; *What you will reap you will sow* (Galatians 6:7). Yet God still holds out a loving Hand to them:

"Sow for yourselves in acts of loving kindness, reap according to loving kindness . . ."
(Hosea 10:12)

He shows His compassion to them, with this famous verse in Hosea:

"When Israel was a child I loved him, and called My Son out of Egypt."
(Hosea 11:1)

Although this is an allusion to *Jesus* and we see it quoted in Matthew 2:15, its primary context is the Israelites being freed from Egyptian slavery. God voices His disappointment on how quickly they turned to pagan idols and how they will soon be in the hands of the Assyrians, a people who they are already naively starting to court. He also reminds them why He thought their desire for a King was not a good one and was going to lead them into all sorts of trouble:

> *"Where is your king now, so he could save you in all your cities? And your judges of whom you said, Give me a king and princes? I gave you a king in My anger and took him away in My wrath."*
> (Hosea 13:10–11)

One final plea from Hosea ends the book, but you sense it is going to go unheeded:

> *"O Israel, return to the LORD your God for you have fallen because of your iniquity. Take words with you and turn to the LORD! Say to Him, Take away all iniquity and take us graciously, so we will render the words of our lips as sacrificial bulls. Assyria will not save us, we will not ride on horses, neither will we say any longer to the idols, the work of our hands, You are our gods! For in You the fatherless find compassion."*
> (Hosea 14:2–4 – this is Hosea 14:1–3 in other versions)

Then, a reminder for us of God's heart for His people, whether they be Israelites at the time of Hosea or people living in 21st Century Britain:

> *"Who is wise and will understand these things? Prudent and he will know them? For the Ways of the LORD are right, and the just will walk in them, but the transgressors will fall there."*
> (Hosea 14:10 – this is Hosea 14:9 in other versions)

The Book of Isaiah

The big one, the monster book, the deep heart of the Hebrew Scriptures. How to summarise this one, with its many themes and directions? It explores so many issues and is so packed with fulfilled and unfulfilled prophecy that certain liberal commentators suggest that there must have been two or three Isaiahs. In fact, Wikipedia suggests that *virtually no-one* maintains that the entire book was written by the same person, Isaiah. Well, I'm happy to be in the minority that refuses to call God a liar and would even dare to suggest that *the whole Bible* was written by one Person.

The real reason for those "scholarly" conclusions are the rigid Greek structures that can inhabit the mind of a scholar, unwilling to accept that God's Word doesn't necessarily have to follow logical progressions and tidy, expected paths. The *Hebraic mindset* can be hard to grasp for those who fail to understand that biblical writers were a very different kettle of fish to those who work in other genres.

If we're honest, we can't totally blame the scholars. The book really is *all over the place*, skipping regularly from historical narrative, to prophecy spanning four different time frames, that of the impending Judgement of exile, the coming of Jesus, the return from exile and the second coming of Jesus, followed by the millennial kingdom.

So I'm going to be un-Greek and examine it by theme, rather than by verse. And, because so many of the other prophets also write of impending exile, as a result of the appalling behaviour of the people of Israel and Judah, I'll return to this theme when we examine these prophets. Perhaps God's feelings on this matter can be summarised in this short passage, right at the beginning:

"To what purpose is the great number of your sacrifices to Me? Says the LORD, I am full of the burnt offerings of rams and the fat of fed beasts and I do not delight in the blood of bulls or of lambs or of he goats. When you come to appear before Me, who has required this at your hand, to tread My courts? Bring no more vain offerings. Incense is an abomination to Me. Call no more assemblies on new moon and the Sabbath. I cannot bear wickedness with solemn assembly. My very being hates your new

moons and your appointed feasts. They are a trouble to Me. I am weary to bear them. And when you spread forth your hands, I shall hide My eyes from you. Yes, when you make many prayers, I shall not listen. Your hands are full of blood. Immerse yourselves! Make yourselves clean! Put away the anarchy of your doings from before My eyes! Stop doing evil! Learn to do well! Seek judgment! Relieve the oppressed! Judge the father-less! Plead for the widow!"
(Isaiah 1:11–17)

In this passage God is basically screaming one word, *right-eousness* (tzedekah). Isaiah was taken right to the heart of this need, when he received his commission:

"In the year that king Uzziah died I saw the Lord sitting on a throne, high and lifted up, and His train filled the palace. Above Him stood the seraphim: each one had six wings, with two he covered his face, with two he covered his feet, and with two he flew. And one cried to another and said, Holy! Holy! Holy is the LORD of Hosts! The whole earth is full of His glory! And the posts of the door moved at the voice of the one who cried, and the house was filled with smoke. Then I said, Woe is me! For I am undone because I am a man of unclean lips and I live in the midst of a people of unclean lips, for my eyes have seen the King, the LORD of Hosts."
(Isaiah 6:1–5)

Isaiah has a vision of God. Rather than quaking in his boots (the usual response), he was immediately convicted of his own sinfulness. God's holiness made him think of his own lack of righteousness, a fundamental requirement of those who wish to walk on *The Way*. This tends to happen during authentic revivals, such as the Welsh revival at the start of the 20th Century. Here's an eyewitness account:

". . . I sobbed and cried in the darkness with a vague sense of my own sin and of the terrible doom which awaited me. I had a passionate longing to escape from condemnation and be forgiven . . ."

As we know from our nativity readings at Christmas time, Isaiah has a lot to say about the coming of Jesus. We start with a very famous verse indeed:

> *"Therefore the Lord Himself will give you a sign. Behold, the young woman (virgin) will conceive and bear a son and she will call His name Emanuel."*
> (Isaiah 7:14)

Jewish scholars object to this verse being fulfilled by the virgin birth of Jesus. One objection is that the context indicates that this verse was referring to events at the time of Isaiah.

The fact is that this passage contains two separate prophecies, for two different groups of people. The reason we know this is through investigating the Hebrew grammar, in particular the use of *singular* and *plural* words. Without going into complex detail on this, when Isaiah is talking to the King, the words are in the *singular*, but, in verses 13 and 14, he is speaking, in *plural*, to the House of David. So we can envisage the scene. Isaiah is attempting to prophesy to the King, who is being obstructive, so he moves the focus away from the King, uttering an awesome prophecy to the House of David, speaking of a future man, born of a virgin. Having made this proclamation, he returns to the present, finishing his word to the King. So, two prophecies were given, an immediate one to the King and his current concerns and a future one to the House of David.

> *"For unto us a child is born, unto us a Son is given, and the government is upon His shoulder, and His name will be called Wonder, Counselor, Mighty God, Eternal Father, Prince of Peace. Of the increase of His government and Shalom there will be no end, upon the throne of David and upon His kingdom, to order it, and to establish it with judgment and with acts of loving kindness from now even forevermore. The zeal of the* Lord *of Hosts will perform this."*
> (Isaiah 9:5–6 – this is Isaiah 9:6–7 in some versions)

A standard Jewish response to this is that these titles do not refer to Jesus, as he was never called any of these titles during his lifetime. Actually, that's not the point, as these titles are names given to both God and the Promised One himself in Jewish writings. It is clear that the Promised One is being referred to as he will *reign on David's throne*, a necessary condition for Messiah-ship. So this passage could be paraphrased, *"For to us a child is born . . . and he will be God Himself . . ."* So the point is not that this couldn't be Jesus specifically referred to, but that, if Jesus has a claim to be the Promised One, then he would also need to be God Himself.

These titles are known as the "throne names" of the Messiah, the Promised One. Jewish commentators generally state that these titles belong either to God Himself, or to a Jewish contemporary – King Hezekiah is the usual suspect. But Ibn Ezra, one of the greatest biblical commentators of all, refused to follow the party line and stated explicitly that these were all the names of this child of the future. This child who would grow up to be the man who would be God.

> *"And there will come forth a shoot out of the trunk of Jesse, and a Branch will grow out of his roots: and the Spirit of the* Lord *will rest upon Him, the Spirit of 1 wisdom and 2 understanding, the Spirit of 3 counsel and 4 might, the Spirit of 5 knowledge and of the 6 reverence and 7 awe of the* Lord.*"*
> (Isaiah 11:1–2)

The *Branch* is Jesus and what follows are the seven attributes of the Holy Spirit, as you can see indicated in the above passage. Later, Isaiah anticipates John the Baptist announcing Jesus' ministry (see Luke 3:2–6):

> *"A voice announces: In the desert, clear the path for the* Lord*! Make straight in the wilderness a highway for our God! Every valley will be raised and every mountain and hill will be made low, and the crooked*

will be made straight, and the mountain peaks a plain. And the Glory of the LORD *will be revealed, and all flesh will see it together, for the mouth of the* LORD *has spoken it."*
(Isaiah 40:3–5)

This one speaks for itself. Then there are the *suffering servant* passages. They start in Chapter 40 and, in all, a servant is mentioned nineteen times. Although over a half of them are clearly speaking of Israel or the Jewish people, once we reach the climax, in Chapter 53, it is abundantly clear that it is an individual being spoken of:

"For He grew up before Him as a tender plant and as a root out of dry ground. He had no form or splendor, and when we see Him, there is no beauty that we should desire Him. He was despised and rejected by men, a Man of pains and having known about sickness, disease, and as one from Whom men hide their face: He was despised, and we esteemed Him not. Surely He has borne our sicknesses, our pains; He carried them, yet we esteemed Him stricken, smitten of God and afflicted. But He was wounded because of our transgressions, bruised because of our iniquities: the chastisement of our peace was upon Him, and we have been healed by His wounds."
(Isaiah 53:2–5)

A 16th Century rabbi, Moshe Alshekh stated: *"(Our) Rabbis with one voice, accept and affirm the opinion that the prophet is speaking of king Messiah"* (taken from "What the Rabbis know about the Messiah", Rachmiel Frydland, p. 53).

Finally there is Jesus' own calling card, repeated in Luke 4:18–20

"The Spirit of Adonai, the LORD, *is upon me, because the* LORD *has anointed me to preach Good News to the humble. He has sent me to bind up the broken-hearted, to proclaim liberty to the captives, and opening of eyes for those who are bound, to proclaim the acceptable year of the* LORD. *"*
(Isaiah 61:1–2) (Compare Luke 7:18–23)

What a book Isaiah is, how strange these words and ideas must have seemed to him as he conveyed what God had put on his heart! In those passages we see both the promise and the fulfilment of Messiah Jesus. But would we have identified these passages for ourselves, if scholars and theologians hadn't first pointed them out to us? They are not signposted, they are not in a tidy section labelled, *all about the Promised One*. They appear in odd places in Isaiah's meandering series of prophecies, where time flows in many directions and single sentences can span thousands of years. We are simply not trained to think *Hebraically*, as the ancient Jews were. If we were, then this little book, *God's Blueprint*, would not be needed.

The return of the Jewish people to their land may be a contentious issue, but we have already seen it featuring as explicit themes in the books of Joel and Amos. Isaiah mentions it too. Here are two of the main passages:

> *"And it will be in that Day that the remnant of Israel and such as have escaped from the House of Jacob will no longer rely upon him who struck them, but will rely upon the LORD, the Holy One of Israel, in truth. The remnant will return, the remnant of Jacob, to the mighty God. For though Your people Israel are as the sand of the sea, a remnant of them will return: the consumption decreed will overflow with acts of loving kindness."*
> (Isaiah 10:20–22)

> *"And it will be in that Day, the Lord will set His hand again the second time to recover the remnant of His people, which will be left from Assyria, from Egypt, from Patros, from Cush, from Elam, from Shinar, from Hamath, and from the islands of the sea. And He will set up a sign for the nations, and will assemble the outcasts of Israel and gather together the dispersed of Judah from the four corners of the earth."*
> (Isaiah 11:11–12)

This is surely consistent with God's character, as He has so far revealed to us. Although He has been known to turn

His back on some, He will never go against His promises, the Covenant He made all those years previously with Abraham:

> *"And the L*ORD *said to Abram, after Lot was separated from him, "Now lift up your eyes and look northward from the place where you are, then southward and eastward and westward, for I shall give to you and to your seed forever all the land that you see."*
> (Genesis 13:14–15)

We must never forget that there is but *one* Author of the Bible and, whether His mouthpiece is Moses or Isaiah, He will continuously remind us what is chiefly on His heart. His faithfulness to His covenant people is one such concern.

One persistent theme of Isaiah's is when he takes his prophetic telescope and peers into the *far future*, to the End of Days. There are many passages, famous ones. This is where we get the oft-repeated phrases:

> *"And many peoples will go and say, Come and let us go up to the Mountain of the L*ORD *. . ."*
> (Isaiah 2:3)

> *"And He will judge among the nations and will decide among many peoples. And they will beat their swords into plowshares and their spears into pruning hooks. Nation will not lift up sword against nation, neither will they learn war any more".*
> (Isaiah 2:4)

> *". . . but He will judge the poor with righteousness and decide with equity for the humble of the earth and He will strike the earth with the rod of His mouth, and with the breath of His lips He will slay the wicked."*
> (Isaiah 11:4)

"The wolf also will dwell with the lamb and the leopard will lie down with the kid, and the calf and the young lion and the fatling together, and a small youth will lead them."
(Isaiah 11:6)

"Then the eyes of the blind will be opened, and the ears of the deaf will be unstopped. Then the lame man will leap like a deer and the tongue of the mute will sing, for waters will break out in the wilderness and streams in the desert."
(Isaiah 35:5–6)

Of course, we are not there yet, but we are nearer than we were yesterday and a lot closer to it than Isaiah.

So Isaiah was an important prophet, perhaps *the* most important and perhaps this is why, out of all books in the Hebrew Scriptures, it is the centrepiece of the Dead Sea Scrolls exhibit in the Israel Museum in Jerusalem. A complete intact manuscript was found, dating to before the time of Jesus, with virtually identical content to what we find in our modern Bibles. One in the eye for those who think that the Bible has been tampered with, and especially that prophecies for Jesus must have been written by Christians after the event!

We finish with a passage that ought to speak to us, whether we are Israelites worshipping at a dodgy altar, or Jews in Roman occupation yearning for their Messiah, or Christians in the modern age, struggling to maintain a good witness in a world that is hostile or indifferent:

"You must seek the LORD while He may be found, call to Him while He is near. Let the wicked forsake his way and the unrighteous man his thoughts, and let him return to the LORD and He will have mercy upon him; and to our God, for He will abundantly pardon. For My thoughts are not your thoughts, neither are your ways My Ways, says the LORD. For as the heavens are higher than the earth, so are My Ways higher than your ways and My thoughts higher than your thoughts. For as the rain

*and the snow come down from heaven and do not return there, but water
the earth and make it bring forth and bud so it will give seed to the sower
and bread to the eater, so My word will go forth out of My mouth: it will
not return to Me empty-handed, but it will accomplish that which I please
and it will succeed wherever I send it."*
(Isaiah 55:6–11)

The Book of Micah

Here's an interesting one. Micah, who lived in Judah at around
the same time as Isaiah, produced a series of prophecies in
his short book that seems to say it all. Virtually every area we
have already explored, is covered in these seven chapters.
Micah is the prophet in the pocket, the sound-byte proclaimer,
perhaps more suited to "attention deficient" modern readers
than any other of his associates. Read this book and, within
an hour or so you will get a very good summary of the *heart
of God*.

He first lays into those in the Southern Kingdom, who seem
to be going the same ways as their northern counterparts:

*"For the transgression of Jacob is all this and for the sins of the House
of Israel. What is the transgression of Jacob? Is it not Samaria? And
what are the high places of Judah? Are they not Jerusalem? . . . For her
wound is incurable, for it has come to Judah. It has come to the gate of
My people, to Jerusalem."*
(Micah 1:5, 9)

By now the Northern Kingdom, Israel (Jacob) has been
conquered and deported by the Assyrians (or it is about to
happen). Can't they see how Israel is *reaping what it had
sown*? Again, the familiar refrain, *don't they know Who they are
dealing with*?

Micah has a particularly biting indictment of his fellow
"prophets":

"Thus says the LORD concerning the prophets who make My people err, who bite with their teeth and cry, Shalom! And he who does not put into their mouths, they even prepare war against him. Therefore it will be night for you, so you will not have a vision, and it will be dark for you, so you will not divine and the sun will go down over the prophets and day will be dark over them. Then the seers will be ashamed and the diviners confounded. Yes, they will all cover their lips for there is no answer from God."
(Micah 3:5–7)

He then displays his credentials as a true mouthpiece of God by reminding us that at least he is castigating Israel for its sin. He is not *prophesying for money* or claiming false divine ownership for their words (Read Micah 3:11).

How many modern prophets fall into that category? How many of them are living up to God's calling by castigating the Church for its sin, rather than following their own personal agendas by preaching prosperity, revival and anything else that tickles the ear and opens the wallet?

Micah then peers forwards to the Last Days in Chapter 4, with a view of the future Kingdom that could have been lifted from the very pages of Isaiah, with such familiar phrases as *they will beat their swords into plowshares and their spears into pruning hooks. Nation will not lift up sword against nation nor will they learn war any more.*

He then deftly reduces the focus and predicts the exile of Judah into Babylon, a full 200 years before it actually happens:

"Be in pain and labor to bring forth, O daughter of Zion, like a woman in travail, for now you will go forth out of the city and you will dwell in the field and you will go even to Babylon . . ."
(Micah 4:10)

Then he hits us with the verse that gets most of us flicking anxiously through uncharted waters in our Bibles at Christmas times. *Now where do I find the Book of Micah, I haven't read it since last Christmas!?*

> *"But you, Bethlehem Ephratah, though you are little among the thousands of Judah, yet out of you One will come forth to Me Who is to be ruler in Israel, Whose goings forth are from of old, from everlasting."*
> (Micah 5:1 – this is Micah 5:2 in other versions)

Well I didn't see that one coming! As we saw with Isaiah, we shouldn't expect the narrative to flow predictably and in date order. They wrote it as they saw it. We mustn't prod and analyse, just accept every word as an expression of God's heart to His people. Perhaps He wanted this important verse to stand out, as a mountain peak of revelation, surrounded by valleys of narrative and prophecy.

This revelation then gives way to a discussion of the dispersion of Israel, then this:

> *"And it will be in that Day, says the LORD, that I will cut off your horses from your midst and I shall destroy your chariots . . . And I shall execute vengeance in anger and fury upon the nations who did not obey."*
> (Micah 5:9–14 – this is Micah 5:10–15 in other versions)

The *Day of the* LORD, that day in the future that signals the wrapping up of things, a persistent feature in the prophetic writings. And, at an undeterminable time before that, the return of the Jews to their ancestral home:

> *"**Do not rejoice against me, O my enemy!** When I fall, I shall rise. When I sit in darkness, the LORD will be a light to me. I shall bear the indignation of the LORD because I have sinned against Him. Until He pleads my cause and executes justice for me, He will bring me out to the light and I shall behold His acts of loving kindness. Then she that is my enemy will see and shame will cover her who said to me, Where is the LORD your God? My eyes will behold her. Now she will be trod down like*

the mire of the streets. The day that your walls are to be built, that appointed day, is yet far removed.".
(Micah 7:8–11)

And hidden within this small gem of a book, is a small gem of a verse,

"He has shown you, O man, what is good. **And what does the** L<small>ORD</small> **require of you, but to do justice, to love loving kindness, and to walk humbly with your God?!"**
(Micah 6:8)

For the editor of the *One New Man Bible* this is deemed one of the most significant verses in the Bible. It's so important to God, that *it is shouted*. It's important because it is the embodiment of *The Way*, the way we are meant to be, the way we are meant to respond to His Word. We are called to do justice, to love loving kindness and to walk humbly with our God.

Micah is a very neglected prophet, so if you have an hour to spare . . . ?

The warrior and the poet

The First Book of Chronicles

This is very much a recap before we move on, a rewind to the events leading up to the time of King David. In fact it is the history of the first few thousand years of mankind, from Adam to David's early descendants. It is also revision, as most of it we've read before, in Genesis, 1 & 2 Samuel and 1 Kings. The *Chronicles* are also the last books of the Hebrew Scriptures to be written, a backward glance at what has come earlier. So what's new? There's *always new*, God always has something new for us and what will be new for me, will hopefully be new or fresh to you, too.

Being dominated by a mass of genealogies, covering the main players but also the bit-parts, it also provides snippets of narratives, fleshing out the stories behind the names, particularly in the second half of the book. What we will do is to concentrate on one character, or should I say, *The Main Character*. Let's see where God has seen fit to interact with His creation and what this can tell us about Him in the process.

He first appears in a very interesting and *controversial* passage:

"And Jabez was more honorable than his brothers and his mother called his name Jabez, saying, because I bore him with sorrow. And Jabez called

on the God of Israel saying, Oh that You would bless me indeed and enlarge my border, and that Your hand would be with me, and that You would keep me from evil, so it would not grieve me! And God granted him that which he requested."
(1 Chronicles 4:9–10)

Controversial because *that* prayer of Jabez became *The Prayer of Jabez*, a multi-million dollar phenomenon, spanning books and small group studies, with the sales pitch,

Are you ready to reach for the extraordinary? To ask God for the abundant blessings He longs to give you? Join Dr Bruce Wilkinson to discover how the remarkable prayer of a little-known Bible hero can release God's favor, power and protection. You'll see how one daily prayer can help you leave the past behind – and break through to the life you were meant to live.

Can God's blessings be triggered by a daily prayer? Does this come out of a true relationship with the living God or does this reduce Him to a *genie in the lamp*, compelled to act according to a regular invocation? Is this what God had in mind when adding this little story within the genealogy of Judah or was it just simply an encouragement to us that God does answer prayer and supply our needs when we honour Him and desire blessings for the right reasons and motivations?

Let's move from a 21st Century marketing re-imagining and get back to the nitty-gritty of God involving Himself in the affairs of man:

". . . for they cried to God in the battle and He was entreated by them because they put their trust in Him . . . For many fell down slain, because the war was of God . . . And they acted faithlessly against the God of their fathers and went astray after the gods of the peoples of the land, whom God destroyed before them."
(1 Chronicles 5:20, 22, 25)

God was the reason for all victories in war. That's how involved He was. Is there any reason to believe otherwise today or has He put away His *tin helmet and musket?*

> *"So Saul died for his treachery which he committed against the LORD, against the word of the LORD, which he did not keep and also for asking counsel of one who had a familiar spirit, to inquire of it; and did not inquire of the LORD therefore He slew him and turned the kingdom to David the son of Jesse."*
> (1 Chronicles 10:13–14)

So God can not only take out armies, but also Kings that had been divinely anointed. He is no respecter of persons, though He honours those who honour Him . . .

> *"Therefore all the elders of Israel came to the king in Hebron and David made a covenant with them in Hebron before the LORD and they anointed David king over Israel, according to the word of the LORD by Samuel."*
> (1 Chronicles 11:3)

He breaks Kings, but He also makes them. And when He is with you, He is *with you indeed* . . .

> *"So David grew greater and greater, for the LORD of Hosts was with him . . . And they set themselves in the midst of that parcel and delivered it and slew the Philistines and the LORD delivered them by a great deliverance."*
> (1 Chronicles 11:9, 14)

But the reverse also holds. You simply *do not* take Him for granted . . .

> *"And the anger of the LORD was kindled against Uzza and He smote him, because he put his hand on the Ark: and there he died before God."*
> (1 Chronicles 13:10)

Neither do you take for granted those whom He ordains for a special purpose . . .

"And David's reputation went out into all lands and the LORD brought that fear of him upon all the nations."
(1 Chronicles 14:17)

But even "special ones" like King David can still get things very wrong. The key, though, to a sustained relationship with God, is immediate and willing acceptance of one's sins and a real sincere repentance. This is why David was God's favourite. He messed up, as in his dalliance with Bathsheba and his taking of the census, and paid dearly for these lapses. But he was *restored*. Because that's what God does with His people, He is always holding out His Hands to us . . .

"And God was displeased at this thing, therefore He struck Israel. And David said to God, I have sinned greatly, because I have done this thing, but now: Now, please! Take away the iniquity of Your servant! For I have done very foolishly."
(1 Chronicles 21:7–8)

And we need to stay close to Him . . .

"And you, Solomon my son, Know the God of your father and serve Him with your whole heart and with a willing mind, for the LORD searches all hearts and understands all the imaginations of the thoughts. If you seek Him, He will be found by you, but if you forsake Him, He will cast you off forever. Take heed now, for the LORD has chosen you to build a House for the Sanctuary. Be strong! Do it!"
(1 Chronicles 28:9–10)

This shows us that it's not enough just doing good works, even serving Him with a smile, it's *what's in the heart* that matters. It is as true now as it was at the time of David and

Solomon. We can fool each other, you can fool your pastor or your congregation, but *you can't fool God*. He knows what truly motivates you and whether your heart is really in your actions.

But there's no fooling around. If you turn your back on Him, you are opening yourself up to the possibility that He'll do the same with you. How that plays out has occupied the thoughts of theologians and writers for centuries and the best way to approach this is perhaps to fear the worst and *not to put the Lord to the test!*

Then there's the more welcoming flip side to this. We are not all chosen to build a Temple, but we are called to respect our own personal temples of the Holy Spirit living within us and, with these new bodies, help to build up the Body of Christ, wherever God takes us.

"And the Lord *magnified Solomon exceedingly in the sight of all Israel and bestowed upon him such royal majesty as had not been on any king before him in Israel."*
(1 Chronicles 29:25)

And that's something to aspire to!

The Book of Psalms

Now here's a challenge. How to do justice to the 150 poems in the largest book in the Hebrew Scriptures, without being over-selective or over-general? Not having a poetic nature adds to the challenge. *But God can use us despite all of our weaknesses*, I convinced myself as I turned to the beginning of the book.

Now the Psalms are divided up into five collections and one of the first things I noticed was a difference between the first two collections (or books), that is between the first forty one Psalms and the next thirty one. So what criteria did I use? Well, the first collection seemed more intimate, with the author making frequent use of God's divine name, *YHWH* (depicted as Lord), rather than the more distant *Adonai* (depicted as God). Also there were more references to *The Way*, this thread that runs through all of the Hebrew Scriptures, stressing our true purpose, the way that we *act on God's Word*. Finally, there is much more emphasis (shown by bold text in the *One New Man Bible*), indicating that there were times that the author really wanted to **shout** those inspiring words. One Psalm that emphasises all three of these observations is Psalm 25:

*"A psalm of David. Unto You, Lord, do I lift up my soul. O my God, I trust in You. **Do not let me be ashamed! Do not let my enemies triumph over me!** Yea, no one who waits on You will be ashamed. They will be ashamed who act deceitfully without cause! Show me Your Ways, Lord! Teach me Your paths. Lead me in Your truth and teach me, for You are the God of my salvation. On You do I wait all the day. Remember, Lord, Your compassion and Your loving kindnesses, for they have been ever of old. **Do not remember the sins of my youth or my transgressions!** According to Your loving kindness remember me for Your goodness' sake, Lord. Good and upright is the Lord: therefore He will teach sinners in the Way. He will guide the humble in judgment and He will teach the humble His Way. All the paths of the Lord are loving kindness and truth for such as keep His covenant and His testimonies. For Your name's sake, Lord, pardon my iniquity, for it is great. What man is he who reveres the Lord? He will teach him in the Way that He will choose. His inner being will dwell at ease, and his seed will inherit the earth. The secret of the Lord is with those who revere Him, and He will show them His covenant. My eyes are ever toward the Lord, for He will pluck my feet out of the net. Turn to me, and be gracious to me, for I am desolate and afflicted. The troubles of my heart are enlarged. O bring me out of my distresses. Look upon my affliction and my pain, and forgive all my sins. Consider my enemies, for they are many and they hate me with cruel hatred. O keep my life and deliver me. **Do not let me be put to shame!** For I put my trust in You. Let integrity and uprightness preserve me, for I hope in You. Redeem Israel, O God, out of all his troubles."*

It's written by someone who, in short, just wants to do the right thing by his God. It reads like an intimate exchange between Father and son, with the latter pleading for restitution and realignment. Well, we know who that person was, as he's identified. It's *King David* and we have already determined that as flawed as this man was, he was always quick to identify his sins and seek to get right with God. The consequences of failure to do so were made only too clear to him and we should strive to learn from the painful lessons of David's life.

The first forty-one Psalms were mostly written by King David, ending the collection with the emphatic flourish, *Amen and Amen.* The next few Psalms, where the emphasis and theme seem to change, had a different author, the *Sons of Korah.* Now where have we heard that name before, *Korah?* He was the chap at the time of Moses who rebelled and was swallowed up in the ground for his troubles. The very same man. But God spared his sons, as He had plans for his descendants. Seven generations after Korah we get the prophet Samuel and then, not long after that, we have the *Sons of Korah,* the great tabernacle and Temple singers and musicians and writers of some twenty five Psalms. This little vignette shows us that one bad apple doesn't have to ruin the whole barrel. Out of the worst kind of rebellion against God, came a genealogical line that produced anointed prophets and musicians. There are many such stories these days of great exploits and acts of altruism coming from the children of Nazis and the such.

So the Psalms had a few different authors. There is one Psalm though that had a very special author, this is Psalm 90, the only one generally agreed to have been written by *Moses* himself. Let's read this together and see what it can tell us about the great man.

"A prayer of Moses the man of God. My Lord, You have been our dwelling place in all generations. Before the mountains were brought forth, or You

had ever birthed the earth and the world, even from everlasting to everlasting, You are God. You turned man to destruction and said, Return, you children of men. For a thousand years in Your sight are but as yesterday when it is past, and as a watch in the night: You carried them away as with a flood. They are as asleep, in the morning they are like grass which grows up. In the morning it flourishes and grows up; in the evening it is cut down and withers. For we are consumed by Your anger and we are troubled by Your wrath. You have set our iniquities before Yourself, our secrets in the light of Your countenance. For all our days are declined in Your wrath: we spend our years as a thought. The days of our years are threescore years and ten, and by reason of strength they are fourscore years, yet is their pride, labor, and sorrow, for it is soon cut off and we fly away. Who knows the power of Your anger? Even according to Your awe, so is Your wrath. So teach us to number our days so we can apply our hearts to wisdom. Return! LORD, how long? And be compassionate concerning Your servants. O satisfy us early with Your loving kindness, so we can rejoice and be glad all our days. Make us glad according to the days in which You have afflicted us, the years in which we have seen evil. Your work will appear to Your servants and Your glory to their children. And let the pleasantness, favor of the Lord our God be upon us and You establish the work of our hands upon us, yea, You establish the work of our hands."

Not as intimate as David's psalm, not so much a sense of the partnership between man and God, but rather one between God and His corporate people, a nation that needed to be forged in righteousness. We see here a reminder of our mortality and utter dependence on God, Who determines the paths of mankind and even the lengths of our days. It's a plea for divine involvement and whereas David was a man more caught up in his own failings, Moses was one who spent his days surrounded by a large assembly of flawed people, with sins often exercised and punishments ever apparent. So, whereas David's psalms have a lot of "I"s and "me"s, this one of Moses is very much about "we" and "us".

Finally, it is interesting to contrast the first and the last Psalm. Psalm 1, which could have been written by David (or even Solomon), concentrates on man and his actions, with a stark contrast of the fate of the godly and the ungodly. The very first line is:

"Blessed is the man who does not walk in the counsel of the ungodly, or stand in the way of sinners, or sit in the seat of the scornful."
(Psalm 1:1)

And the last line:

"For the Lord *knows the Way of the righteous, but the way of the ungodly will perish."*
(Psalm 1:6)

All good theology, stuff for the "head". The final psalm, Psalm 150, is unashamedly God-centred, "heart" stuff, traditionally written by King David. Perhaps we can visualise him as a young shepherd dancing joyfully in the fields, exclaiming these words:

"HalleluYah! Praise God in His Sanctuary! Praise Him in the firmament of His power! Praise Him for His mighty acts! Praise Him according to His excellent greatness! Praise Him with the sound of the shofar! Praise Him with the lute and harp! Praise Him with the tambourine and dance! Praise Him with stringed instruments and flutes! Praise Him upon the loud cymbals! Praise Him upon the high sounding cymbals! Everyone who has breath will praise the Lord*! HalleluYah!"*

If only life were so simple and uncomplicated these days!

As Christians, there is one aspect of the Psalms that should excite us and that is what they tell us about the coming Messiah, or, to be specific, *the life and death of Jesus Christ*. It is not laid out in a group of Psalms, but, consistent with the way God has sprinkled His Messianic gems throughout the Hebrew

Scriptures, we see the whole story, if we look hard enough. Here are some extracts strung together. I urge you to check them out for yourself to ensure that I haven't pulled them out of context. How could this not speak of Jesus?

> *I shall declare the decree: the LORD said to me, You are My Son. This day I have begotten You. (Psalm 2:7) . . . I shall open my mouth in a parable. (Psalm 78:2) . . . But I am a worm and not a man; a reproach of men and despised by the people. (Psalm 22:6) . . . You have known my reproach and my shame and my dishonor: my adversaries are all before You. Reproach has broken my heart and I am sick: and I looked for some to take pity, but there was no one, and for comforters, but I found no one. (Psalm 69:20–21) . . . in My thirst they gave me vinegar to drink. (Psalm 69:22) . . . I am poured out like water and all My bones are out of joint. (Psalm 22:15) . . . They part My garments among them and cast lots for My clothing. (Psalm 22:19) . . . My God, My God, why have You utterly forsaken Me? Why are You so far from helping Me, from the words of My groaning? (Psalm 22:2) . . . For You will not commit My life to the grave, neither will You permit Your Pious One to see corruption. (Psalm 16:10) . . . You have ascended on high: You have led captivity captive: You have taken gifts among men, yea, even among the rebellious, so Yah, God, might dwell among them. (Psalm 68:19) . . . The LORD says to my Lord, Sit at My right hand until I make Your enemies Your footstool. (Psalm 110:1) . . . The LORD has sworn and He will not repent, You are a priest forever after the order of Melchizedek. (Psalm 110:4) . . . I have made a covenant with My chosen, I have sworn to David My servant, I shall establish your seed forever and build up your throne to all generations. Selah. (Psalm 89:4–5) . . . So the nations and all the kings of the earth will revere the name of the LORD Your glory. When the LORD will build up Zion, He will appear in His glory. He will regard the prayer of the destitute and not despise their prayer. This will be written for the generation to come, and the people that will be created will praise the LORD (Psalm 102:16–19).*

It's a strong case laid out here. Perhaps this is a good time for quiet contemplation?

Wisdom and folly

The Second Book of Chronicles

More revision time, as, on first glance, this book is another look at material we have already seen in 1 Kings and 2 Kings. But, in a few places, a lot more is filled in *between the lines*, to stories fairly whisked through in those earlier books. One such story is the saga of King Asa. Here's a summary of what we know about him from 1 Kings 15:9–24.

He reigned forty-one years in Jerusalem, as King of Judah and generally did the right thing, in banishing prostitutes, his father's idols and his pagan mother. But he left the high places alone. His story, though, is dominated by one series of events, his covenant with Ben-Hadad of Syria, sealed with the treasures from God's Temple and the King's house. He did this so that Syria would switch allegiances from the Northern Kingdom of Israel to Judah and attack them on his behalf. This policy was successful – militarily speaking. Asa eventually died in old age of some foot disease.

It would be good to find out more about this intriguing man, particularly how his early dedication to God wasn't sustained in his later years. The story is fleshed out more in 2 Chronicles 14:1 to 16:14, three whole chapters devoted to this King. We first read exactly how he not only cleansed the Kingdom at the start of his reign but encouraged his people to follow the Torah.

As a reward for these acts, God gave Judah sufficient peace that Asa had time to fortify many of the cities. He also built up an impressive army, which had a very remarkable success in a battle with the million strong army of Zerah the Ethiopian. This success was sealed by his attitude:

> *"And Asa cried to the LORD his God and said, LORD, it is nothing with You to help, whether the mighty or the powerless. Help us, LORD our God! For we rest in You and we go against this multitude in Your name. LORD, You are our God!* ***Do not let man prevail against You!"***
> (2 Chronicles 14:10 – this is 2 Chronicles 14:11 in other versions)

The Ethiopian army was decimated and there was a great deal of spoil taken back to Jerusalem. Things were going well, but perhaps God sensed a subtle change in the King, because He sent the prophet Azariah to speak to him, so:

> *"Listen to me, Asa, and all Judah and Benjamin. The LORD is with you, while you are with Him and if you seek Him, He will be found by you, but if you forsake Him, He will forsake you."*
> (2 Chronicles 15:2)

This worked and the King slipped into revival mode, destroying more pagan idols that had crept into usage and offered God a massive sacrifice from the spoils of war with the Ethiopians.

> *"And they entered a covenant to seek the LORD God of their fathers with all their heart and with all their inner being, that whoever would not seek the LORD God of Israel should be put to death, whether small or great, whether man or woman. And they swore to the LORD with a loud voice, and with shouting and with trumpets and with shofars. And all Judah rejoiced at the oath, for they had sworn with all their heart and sought Him with their whole desire and He was found by them, and the LORD gave them rest all around."*
> (2 Chronicles 15:12–15)

The episode with Ben-Hadad of Syria came around five years before the end of his reign. We now read what God thought about this *covenant* with Syria. He sent the prophet Hanani to have a quiet word with the King. He reminded him of the great success God had given him against the Ethiopians, *so why are you now relying on the king of Syria and not on the* LORD *your God, eh?*

Asa's reaction was *very* different to when Azariah had spoken to him. He threw a strop and threw Hanani into prison and all we read next is that *Asa oppressed some of the people at the same time* (2 Chronicles 16:10). How sad and how stupid!

He was even more stupid when, three years later, he contracted this disease of his feet, *yet in his disease he did not seek the* LORD, *but the physicians* (2 Chronicles 16:12). That's an interesting one, as we are guilty of the same thing, admittedly influenced by the superb skill-set of modern doctors. Yet, how many of us, when given a choice between the two, go for modern medicine?

When he died, his son *Jehoshaphat* took over. Interestingly 1 Kings gives virtually no information about him, but, in 2 Chronicles, we have a very interesting picture painted.

He starts off well, as many of them do:

> "And the LORD was with Jehoshaphat, because he walked in the first Ways of his father David and did not seek baalim, but sought the God of his father and walked in His commandments, and not after the doings of Israel."
> (2 Chronicles 17:3–4)

Jehoshaphat walked in *The Way*, which means that he took the Torah seriously. As a result, God looked down with favour on him, particularly as he sent teachers and priests throughout the kingdom, teaching Torah. This worried the pagan nations and some of them even brought gifts, reminiscent of the days of Solomon. Jehoshaphat accordingly grew very rich and powerful.

What could possibly go wrong? Well . . .

"Now Jehoshaphat had riches and honor in abundance and joined affinity with Ahab."
(2 Chronicles 18:1)

Surely this can't be *the* Ahab, who worshipped Baal, married the dreadful Jezebel and persecuted Elijah? The same. Ahab wanted him to join forces in war against Ramoth-Gilead and Jehoshaphat exclaimed:

". . . I am as you are and my people as your people, and we will be with you in the war."
(2 Chronicles 18:3)

Rather naïve of him, don't you think? Their differences became apparent when Ahab was asked to fetch a prophet to see what God was counselling. He only had a dodgy bunch at hand and refused to fetch the only true prophet at his disposal, *Micaiah*, whom he hated! So the prophets all spoke and predicted victory. It was Micaiah's turn to speak and . . . he agreed with the others! Ahab was suspicious.

"And the king said to him, How many times will I swear to you that you say nothing but the truth to me in the name of the LORD?"
(2 Chronicles 18:15)

It's interesting that Ahab in his heart knew that Micaiah only ever spoke truth. So he pressed him further and Micaiah admitted that God wanted Ahab to suffer defeat and so put lying spirits in the mouths of all the dodgy prophets (what did you expect, after all, I did call them *dodgy* prophets?).

Micaiah was sent away to prison and the two kings went off to Ramoth-Gilead. The cowardly Ahab disguised himself in battle but Jehoshaphat was identified by the enemy (thinking he was Ahab), but they were stopped in their tracks by God, Who knew His friends. Ahab was killed by a fortuitous arrow in the joints of his armour. God also knew *His* enemies.

Jehoshaphat went home and was castigated by Hanani the seer for his poor judgement, but was given a fresh start on account of his earlier zeal for God. He then set up righteous judges throughout the land and paid particular attention to Jerusalem, ensuring that God was to be firmly at the centre of Temple life.

Then came the Moabites and Ammonites and Jehoshaphat's worthy response was to declare a fast and to seek the Lord. He reminded God that these were the very two nations that the Israelites under Moses were told not to invade. *Has this decision come back to haunt them?* Then God answered:

> "Listen, all Judah, and you inhabitants of Jerusalem and you king Jehoshaphat, Thus says the LORD to you, **Do not be in awe! Do not be dismayed because of this great multitude!** For the battle is not yours, but God's."
>
> (2 Chronicles 20:15)

They were not to worry, or even make battle plans. Instead the singers and musicians were to go out before the army to praise God! And while they were doing this, battle commenced, with complete victory and three days gathering of spoils. The fourth day they held a holy assembly and blessed the Lord. Then they returned to their homes, singing and rejoicing. Now that's how wars should be fought! How many armies in history have claimed God's blessings and insisted on the rightness of their cause? And how many of them went into battle so convinced of this that they rejoiced before the Lord even before the battle, *celebrating a sure victory in advance?* Very few, I would suggest.

For the battle is not yours, but God's.

Perhaps this is true in all cases? We always need to know, in all of our battles (in all areas of our lives), where the Lord stands. Because that's where the victory will be, though it may not always be apparent at the time.

The Book of Proverbs

There is today a "ministry", promoted heavily on Christian satellite TV, that features a high-profile "teacher" churning out proverbs, supposedly "wisdoms" from his own understandings and very much tied in with the "prosperity gospel". His "wisdom" is to be contrasted with God's wisdom, the clever little collection that we find in the Book of Proverbs:

> *"Reverence of the* LORD *is the instruction of wisdom, and humility is before honor."*
> (Proverbs 15:33)

So, humility comes before honour, and yet today we see not a shred of humility in many of today's TV teachers, for whom personal glorification seems to be a perpetual need. Reverence of the LORD is sadly missing, as the accent of the ministry is on individual gain, whether financial, social or personal circumstance.

We really don't need *man's* wisdom and the best place for practical pointers of *God's* wisdom is the book of Proverbs, which is free to everyone.

So what is the Book of Proverbs? It is basically a collection of . . . proverbs, mostly written by King Solomon. They are chiefly on the theme of *wisdom*, with the aim of promoting godly values, moral behaviour and the right conduct. They are very much practical signposts for *The Way*.

Bearing in mind that there are eight collections of proverbs in the book, with each featuring scores of individual sayings, how can I say anything meaningful, with so much to choose from? What I have done is to pick a few out, because they are relevant to me and hopefully to you too. Let us begin.

"Reverence of the LORD *is the beginning of knowledge. Fools despise wisdom and instruction."*
(Proverbs 1:7)

That's very similar to the one already quoted. Its very essence is our need to trust that God knows best and that, in the first instance, our knowledge and the wisdom that flows from it, should flow from His Word. Otherwise we are just fools. In fact, we are really saying that *everyone in our World* is a fool unless they are acting in godly wisdom. Try telling that to your local MP, the next time you visit him.

"Do not let loving kindness and truth forsake you! *Bind them about your neck! Write them upon the tablet of your heart, so you will find favor and good understanding in the sight of God and man."*
(Proverbs 3:3–4)

The Way is when mind and heart work in perfect harmony, when the truth of God's Word leads us into acts of loving kindness. This is so important that we need constant reminders and, when we get things right, we will find favour with both God and man, which can't be bad!

"My son, **Do not despise the chastening of the LORD!** *Neither be weary of His correction, for whom the* LORD *loves He corrects, even as a father the son in whom he delights."*
(Proverbs 3:11–12)

We are a wilful bunch really, even those who have *trod the path* for many years. If you have not felt the LORD's corrections, then you ain't doing it right, because it's probably more a case of *ignoring* the LORD's corrections. We must never be too proud to accept a bit of chastening now and again, even when God allows others (such as your wife!) to apply the *necessary encouragement* (and the ointment afterwards!)

*"The beginning of wisdom is, Acquire wisdom! And with all you have
gotten get understanding."*
(Proverbs 4:7)

Clumsily expressed but a simple sentiment. We need to
actively try to improve ourselves and if that means switching
over TV channels from the soap to the documentary, then that's
a good start!

*"The LORD hates these six things, and seven are an abomination to Him:
a proud look, a lying tongue, hands that shed innocent blood, a heart
that devises wicked imaginations, feet that are swift in running to evil,
a false witness who speaks lies, and the one who sows discord among
brothers."*
(Proverbs 6:16–19)

It's good to know what particularly irks the LORD. So if you're
a proud, lying, murderer who plots and plans, gossips and stirs
up trouble, then expect big problems as He considers you an
abomination. Of course it would be most wise if you were *none*
of these seven things.

*"Folly is a clamorous woman. She is simple and knows nothing. For she
sits at the door of her house, on a seat in the high places of the city, to
call passengers who go right on their ways: whoever is simple, let him
turn in here: and as for him who wants understanding, she says to him,
Stolen waters are sweet, and bread eaten in secret is pleasant. But he does
not know that the dead are there; her guests are in the depths of hell."*
(Proverbs 9:13–18)

What an evocative scene! The temptation to be distracted
from the right Way can be strong when enticements are put
before us, especially simple, uncomplicated ones that may seem
harmless. But harmless they are *not* and the road to hell is paved
with such intentions!

"Hatred stirs up strifes but love covers all transgressions."
(Proverbs 10:12)

There are circumstances where it is a whole lot easier to hate than to love, but only love has true power.

"The wicked makes a deceitful reward, but a sure reward will be for the one who sows acts of loving kindness."
(Proverbs 11:18)

"In the Way of acts of loving kindness is life, and in its pathway there is no death."
(Proverbs 12:28)

The world can bestow all sorts of rewards on you, according to the ever-changing rules of conduct in our society. But acts of loving kindness are eternally worthy and these provide us with the only reward worth attaining.

"Better is a little with acts of loving kindness than great revenues without justice."
(Proverbs 16:8)

"It is better to be of a humble spirit with the lowly, than to divide the spoil with the proud."
(Proverbs 16:19)

Wouldn't we all prefer to be a kind (but poor) nurse than a rich arrogant banker? Not that all nurses are kind and all bankers are arrogant, but the way that we act is what *really* defines us in God's eyes, not our position in life and the money we earn.

"Do not say, I will repay evil! Wait on the LORD and He will save you."
(Proverbs 20:22)

It is our basic nature to repay evil in short-term ways that seem best to us (e.g. a punch on the nose) but if we leave it in God's hands, He will certainly deal with this in the long-term, even if you are not around to witness the outcome.

> *"Every way of a man is right in his own eyes, but the* Lord *ponders the hearts. To do acts of loving kindness and justice is more acceptable to the* Lord *than sacrifice."*
> (Proverbs 21:2–3)

This is so key to our whole story. It's the final bit that's often neglected, even by Christians today. God is happier if we spent the next hour visiting a needful person rather than reading yet another book on how to be a good Christian (apart from my books, of course).

> *"Train up a child in the Way he should go and when he is old, he will not depart from it."*
> (Proverbs 22:6)

This is about bringing up children in Christian love, following *The Way* of obedience that has wound its way purposefully through Scripture, rather than in the kind of dry ritual and lip-service that breeds resentment and welcome release when they leave home.

And talking of homes and such matters. Here is a proverb in the section entitled, *The Virtuous Woman* and I think of the wonderful woman that the Lord has blessed me with over the last thirty four years:

> *"Who can find a virtuous woman? For her price is far above pearls . . . She will do him good and not evil all the days of her life."*
> (Proverbs 31:10, 12)

And this is where I must end. Well I could go on forever, but

I have to stop somewhere. Of course, you can *always* read the rest of the Proverbs for yourself.

The Book of Zephaniah

Here was a prophet with royal blood (King Hezekiah was his great grandfather) who operated during the reign of one of the better kings of Judah, *Josiah*. This was the King who found the Torah scrolls and brought about a revival in the land, so we can assume that Zephaniah worked closely with the King to bring this about. They had much to do and God spoke very strongly through this prophet about the state of the Nation:

> *"I shall also stretch out My hand over Judah and over all the inhabitants of Jerusalem and I will cut off the remnant of Baal from this place and the name of the idolatrous priests with the priests, and those who worship the host of heaven from the housetops,"*
> (Zephaniah 1:4–5)

The irreversible clock of judgement had already been set, thanks to the monumentally evil behaviour of King Josiah's grandfather, *Manasseh*, who had thoroughly paganised the land during his lengthy fifty five year rule. So there was a lot to undo.

But, before we concentrate on what Zephaniah had to say about God's people, it's worth mentioning what he also had to say about certain pagan nations first. God explodes in wrath against them, for what they did to His people:

> *". . . The word of the LORD is against you, O Canaan, the land of the Philistines, I shall even destroy you, so there will be no inhabitant . . . Surely Moab will be like Sodom and the children of Ammon as Gomorrah, a bush of nettles and salt pits and a perpetual desolation . . . And He will stretch out His hand against the north and destroy Assyria and will make Nineveh a desolation, dry like a wilderness."*
> (Zephaniah 2:5, 9, 13)

There's a finality about these proclamations, but what about His condemnation of *Judah*, His people. Well, it's not good. This is what He has to say about Jerusalem:

> *"Her princes within her are roaring lions, her judges are evening wolves who do not gnaw the bones on the next day. Her prophets are a wanton and treacherous people. Her priests have profaned the Sanctuary, they have done violence to the Torah."*
> (Zephaniah 3:3–4)

But there's a difference in God's attitude to His people and the rest. It's worth repeating a Proverb already examined:

> *"My son, **Do not despise the chastening of the LORD!** Neither be weary of His correction, for whom the LORD loves He corrects, even as a father the son in whom he delights."*
> (Proverbs 3:11–12)

Judgement on Judah is coming, it is called *Babylon*, but, unlike the Ninevites, Philistines, Moabites and Ammonites, it is *not* to be final. It is a *chastening*, the one-word theme of the prophet Zephaniah.

Because . . . the story doesn't end. There is to be a final restoration of Judah. Because He has corrected . . . now He shows His love:

> *"In that Day it will be said to Jerusalem, **Do not fear!** To Zion, **Do not let your hands be slack!** The LORD your God is mighty in your midst! He will deliver! He will rejoice enthusiastically over you with joy! He will rest in His love, He will rejoice over you with singing. I shall gather those who are sorrowful for the solemn assembly, who departed from you, to whom the reproach of it was a burden. Behold, at that time I shall undo all that afflicts you and I will save her who halts and gather her who was driven out, and I will get them praise and fame in every land where they have been put to shame. At that time I shall bring you back, even in the*

time that I gather you. For I shall make you a name and a praise among all the peoples of the earth, when I turn back your captivity before your eyes, says the LORD.*"*
(Zephaniah 3:16–20)

But then there's a reckoning. We usually call it *Armageddon*. When we see the wrath with which God deals with those biblical nations who mistreated His people, the Jews, what do you think will happen to the Gentile nations who have been at it for the good part of 2,000 years?

"Therefore wait on Me, says the LORD, *until the Day that I rise up to the prey, for My determination is to gather the nations so I can assemble the kingdoms to pour My indignation upon them, all My fierce anger, for all the earth will be devoured with the fire of My zeal."*
(Zephaniah 3:8)

It's a sobering thought.

The Book of Nahum

Around about the same time, another prophet was also declaring judgement on the Assyrians. This was Nahum. He was writing at a time when the Assyrian Empire, under *Ashurbanipal* (Asnappar), was undergoing its greatest expansion, now including Babylonia, Persia, Syria and Egypt. Confidence must have been high in the Assyrian court, at the capital, Nineveh. The King must have felt on top of the world. Surely nothing could come in the way of his mighty army?

Well, he was wrong.

"The LORD *is good, a stronghold in the day of trouble and He knows those who trust in Him. But with an overrunning flood He will make an utter end of the place, Nineveh, and darkness will pursue His enemies."*
(Nahum 1:7–8)

Ashurbanipal, along with all military dictators and powerful leaders, from Nimrod to Putin, has only achieved precisely what God has *allowed* them to achieve. And when God says, *enough is enough*, even the mightiest Empire can be pulled apart like dry branches in a hurricane.

> *"Thus says the LORD, though they are powerful and likewise many, yet thus will they be cut down and pass on."*
> (Nahum 1:12)

Nahum assures the people of Judah that Assyria is firmly in God's cross-hairs. So just keep close to God and He'll take care of business.

> *"Behold, upon the mountains are the feet of him who brings Good News, who is declaring Shalom! O Judah, keep your solemn feasts! Perform your vows! For the wicked one will no longer pass through you. He is utterly cut off."*
> (Nahum 2:1 – this is Nahum 1:15 in other versions)

The Assyrian Empire was only going to last for a couple of decades, when civil war tore out the heart and the Babylonians picked up the pieces.

> *"Behold, I am against you, says the LORD of Hosts and I shall uncover your skirts upon your face and I shall show the nations your nakedness and the kingdoms your shame. And I shall cast abominable filth upon you and make you vile and will set you as a dung-hill. And it will be that all they that look upon you will flee from you and say, Nineveh has been laid waste. Who will bemoan her? Where will I seek comforters for you?"*
> (Nahum 3:5–7)

How the mighty have fallen. Now where have we heard that before?

From Judah with sorrow

The Book of Obadiah

The most talked about feature of this tiny book is that there is no agreement as to when this prophet lived and worked. So I have placed it after Nahum because, just as this other prophet railed against the Assyrians, Obadiah had the *Edomites* as his main target. So we will concentrate on themes rather than historic certainties.

Now the Edomites were a people who lost the plot, in much the same way as their "patriarch" did. This was *Esau*, Jacob's elder brother (by minutes), who sold his birth-right and was a hunter and a fighter by nature, a personality generally at odds with the world. He became the archetypal *estranged brother*, a role sadly sustained by the Edomites in their relationship with their brother race, the Israelites.

This was born out by Obadiah's opening statement:

"Thus says Adonai the LORD concerning Edom, We have heard a message from the LORD and an ambassador is sent among the nations, Arise! Let us rise up against her in battle. Behold, I have made you small among the nations, you are greatly despised. The pride of your heart has deceived you, you who dwell in the clefts of the rock, whose habitation is high, who says in his heart, Who will bring me down to the ground? Though you exalt yourself as the eagle and though you set

*your nest among the stars, I shall bring you down from there: the word
of the* LORD.*"*
(Obadiah 1–4)

How had it come to this? Well they didn't help their case in
their first encounter with the Children of Israel at the Exodus:

*"And Moses sent messengers from Kadesh to the king of Edom, Thus says
your brother Israel, "You know all the trouble that has befallen us . . . Let
us pass, I pray you, through your country. We will not pass through the
fields, or through the vineyards, neither will we drink of the water of the
wells. We will go by the king's highway, we will not turn to the right hand
or to the left until we have passed your borders." And Edom said to him,
"You will not pass by me, or I shall come out against you with the sword."*
(Numbers 20:14,17,18)

It seems that the Edomites had long memories and were far
from reconciled with their brothers. Perhaps there was an element
of jealousy, after all if it wasn't for a blind patriarch and a bowl of
soup, perhaps this *chosen nation* status could have been theirs.

They cemented their fate and ultimate demise as a people
for their actions in helping the Babylonians to plunder Jerusalem
and massacre the occupants:

"Remember, LORD, *the children of Edom in the day of Jerusalem, who
said, Raze it. Raze it to its foundation!"*
(Psalm 137:7)

Obadiah speaks of the fate of the Edomites:

*"And the House of Jacob will be a fire and the house of Joseph a flame
and the house of Esau for stubble and they will kindle in them and devour
them. There will not be any remaining of the house of Esau, for the* LORD
has spoken."
(Obadiah 18)

And what is the lesson for us here? Perhaps as Christians we should pay more attention to our fellow brothers and sisters in the Lord. These days there seems to be more that separates us than unites us, and that can't be right. If God seems to be moving in a ministry that, if you were to admit it, is not one of your favourites, isn't it better to bless what God is doing through them rather than not allowing them to pass through your land?

The Book of Jeremiah

Here's a prophet so important that he was commissioned while still in the womb (Jeremiah 1:5). He was a little bit reluctant (as were Moses and Isaiah), declaring *behold, I do not know how to speak, for I am a youth* (presumably this was a long time since leaving the womb!) God reminds him of his calling:

> *"Do not say, I am a youth! You will go to all to whom I shall send you, and you will speak whatever I command you."*
> (Jeremiah 1:7)

Then the Lord reached out and touched Jeremiah's mouth and revealed his destiny as one who would pull down and destroy, throw down, build and plant. He would have authority over the nations and over the kingdoms. This would be no ordinary life.

He was a contemporary of Zephaniah, with a lengthy career stretching back from good King Josiah, right through to the Babylonian captivity. He was a busy prophet, intent on saving as many of his people as he could, before the inevitable. For this he ended up first in the stocks, then in a prison and then thrown into a pit. He wasn't a popular man, thanks to his unpopular message, delivered with passion and insistence:

> *"Seek refuge! Do not stay! For I AM bringing evil from the north and a great destruction. The lion is coming up from his thicket and the destroyer of the nations is on his way. He is going forth from his place to make*

*your land desolate. Your cities will be laid waste, without an inhabitant.
For this, gird with sackcloth, lament and howl, for the fierce anger of the
LORD has not turned back from us."*
(Jeremiah 4:6–8)

*"Therefore thus says the LORD of Hosts, Because you have not listened to
My words, Behold, I shall send and take all the families of the north, says
the LORD, and Nebuchadnezzar the king of Babylon, My servant, and will
bring them against this land and against its inhabitants and against all
these nations round about and will utterly destroy them and make them
an astonishment and a hissing and perpetual desolations."*
(Jeremiah 25:8–9)

The powers-that-be simply weren't interested in this. He was
too much of a . . . *Jeremiah* (hold on, this is where that term
comes from!) They would rather listen to a false prophet such
as Hananiah, who said, *thus says the LORD, I'll bring back the
captives from Babylon within two years.* God was not pleased and
had Jeremiah deliver this message to him:

*"Then the prophet Jeremiah said to Hananiah the prophet, Now listen!
Obey, Hananiah! The LORD has not sent you, but you make this people
trust in a lie. Therefore thus says the LORD, Behold, I shall cast you from
the face of the earth. This year you will die because you have taught
rebellion against the LORD. So Hananiah the prophet died the same year
in the seventh month."*
(Jeremiah 28:15–17)

Lord, deliver us today from false prophets! It seems that He
is more patient with them these days, but perhaps He is testing
our discernment. After all we have the lessons of Jeremiah and
others to follow and learn from. *Those who have ears to hear . . .*

So Judah finally went into exile at the hands of the
Babylonians. Jeremiah always knew this was inevitable, but
never gave up trying to rescue even some of his people. He was

driven by the sheer pain of it: *My insides. My insides! I am pained at my very heart. My heart makes a noise in me, I cannot hold my peace, because you have heard, O my inner being, the sound of the shofar, the alarm of war* (Jeremiah 4:19).

But he even had warnings for those caught up in this exile. Some would be tempted to seek a new life of anonymity in Egypt, where they *would not hear the sound of the shofar.* In other words, leave their destiny behind for the refuge of assimilation. God was firmly against this. **Do not go to Egypt!** (Jeremiah 42:19). Consequences were made clear:

> "For thus says the LORD of Hosts, the God of Israel, As My anger and My fury has been poured upon the inhabitants of Jerusalem, so will My fury be poured upon you, when you enter Egypt and you will be denounced as evil and an astonishment and a curse and a reproach and you will see this place no more."
>
> (Jeremiah 42:18)

Needless to say, some did travel to Egypt and many bore the consequences, particularly those who turned their back on God in order to worship the pagan *queen of heaven.*

There is a constant theme of God's people and Egypt. It has been used as a place of refuge, particularly for the infant Jesus, but, more often than not, it has been a place of disadvantage (Hebrew slaves before Exodus), or faithlessness (Abraham and the Pharaoh). Egypt has been seen as a picture of the world, of a place on the *outside of blessing.*

Like Isaiah before him, Jeremiah prophesised events that spanned centuries, even millennia.

But first there was a ray of hope for those about to be exiled:

> "For thus says the LORD, after seventy years have passed at Babylon I shall visit you and perform My good word toward you, by causing you to return to this place."
>
> (Jeremiah 29:10)

This was a lot longer than the two years prophesised by Hananiah and, as we will see later on, as our story progresses, *it came to pass.*

What also came to pass was another incredible prophecy where Jeremiah looked further ahead to the demise of the Babylonians at the hands of the Persians. And the reason for this destruction is made clear:

> *"Prepare the arrows! Get the shields ready! The* Lord *has raised up the spirit of the kings of the Medes, for His device is against Babylon, to destroy it, because it is the vengeance of the* Lord, *the vengeance for His Temple."*
> (Jeremiah 51:11)

God had not forgotten what the Babylonians had done to His Temple and He was going to make them pay dearly for this.

Jeremiah also spoke of Jesus:

> *"Behold, the days are coming, says the* Lord, *that I shall perform that good thing which I have promised to the House of Israel and to the House of Judah. In those days and at that time I shall cause the Branch (Sprout) of acts of loving kindness to grow up for David and He will execute justice and acts of loving kindness in the land."*
> (Jeremiah 33:14–15)

Even more importantly he explains what the significance of this great event is going to be, in the *only specific passage* in the Hebrew Scriptures that speaks of the *New Covenant.*

> *"Behold, the days are coming, says the* Lord, *that I will cut a renewed covenant with the House of Israel, and with the House of Judah, not according to the covenant that I made with their fathers in the day that I took them by the hand to bring them out of the land of Egypt, My covenant which they broke, although I* am *husbanding them, says the*

LORD. *But this will be the covenant that I shall make with the House of Israel, after those days, says the LORD, I will put My Torah (Teaching) in their inward parts and write it in their hearts and I will be their God and they will be My people. And each person will no longer teach his neighbour and each person his brother saying, Know the LORD, for they will all know Me from the least of them to the greatest of them, says the LORD, for I shall forgive their iniquity and I shall no longer remember their sin.*"

(Jeremiah 31:30–33 – this is Jeremiah 31:31–34 in other versions)

This covenant is made with the Jews, taken from the Houses of Judah and Israel, *not* the Gentiles. For the full story of how the Gentiles join the story you need to read Romans chapters 9 to 11.

Then came the *galut*, the second exile of the Jews to the furthest-most places on the earth. It has been tempting for some Christians to think that this signalled the end of the story for the Jewish people. Well, Jeremiah didn't think so and neither did God:

"*Thus says the LORD, Who gives the sun for a light by day, the ordinances of the moon and of the stars for a light by night, Who breaks the sea so the waves roar: The LORD of Hosts is His name. If those ordinances depart from before Me, says the LORD, the seed of Israel will also forever cease from being a nation before Me. Thus says the LORD, If heaven above can be measured and the foundations of the earth beneath searched out, I shall also cast off all the seed of Israel for all that they have done: the word of the LORD.*"

(Jeremiah 31:34–36 – this is Jeremiah 31:35–37 in other versions)

Notice that this declaration came straight after the one about the *New Covenant*, indicating that, despite appearances and historical setbacks, the Jews are not forgotten by God. History has borne this out and Jeremiah spoke frequently of a future date when the Jews, spread throughout the world, would return:

"In those days the House of Judah will walk with the House of Israel and they will come together out of the land of the north to the land that I have given to your fathers for an inheritance."
(Jeremiah 3:18)

"Therefore, behold, the days are coming, says the LORD, that they will no longer say, the LORD lives, Who brought the children of Israel from the land of Egypt, but the LORD lives Who brought up and led the seed of the House of Israel out of the north country and from all the countries where I had driven them when they will live in their own land."
(Jeremiah 23:7–8)

This is an interesting thought. A miracle **has happened** – the return of the Jews to their land after nearly 2000 years – that has *supplanted* the original defining miracle of the Jewish people, the Exodus from Egypt. We really need to get our heads round *exactly* how much a miracle this return to the land has been. (For more information about this, I refer you to my book, *Outcast Nation*.)

Then, like Isaiah, he had much to say about the final days, of the millennial Kingdom, after Jesus has returned:

"At that time they will call Jerusalem, The Throne of the LORD and all the nations will be gathered to it, to the name of the LORD, to Jerusalem, nor will they walk any more after the imagination of their corrupt heart."
(Jeremiah 3:17)

"Again I shall build you and you will be built, O virgin of Israel, you will again put on your tambourines and will go forth in the dances of those who make merry. You will plant vineyards again on the mountains of Samaria: the planters will plant and will use their fruit. For there will be a day that the Christians on Mount Ephraim will cry, Arise! Rise and go up to Zion to the LORD our God!"
(Jeremiah 31:3–5 – this is Jeremiah 31:4–6 in other versions)

Yes, you did read it right, *Christians*. The Hebrew word *Notsrim*, frequently translated "watchmen" in Bibles, is actually translated as "Christians" in modern Hebrew! All Christians, both Jew and Gentile, will be visiting *their King* in Jerusalem!

So Jeremiah, this incredible prophet, who was selected while still in the womb, has provided us with a set of signposts that span the whole of history, from Babylonian exile to the future Millennium and which tell us that, if God makes a covenant with a people, the stars and the moon will fall out of the sky before He turns His back on them and that their return to their ancestral land is going to be a *miracle of miracles*.

Unfortunately, the world doesn't see it that way. Neither does much of the Church.

The Book of Lamentations

The Hebrew word for this book is short and direct. It is "eikhah" and it means . . . how? How Jewish is that? How? How is it possible? How did it happen? And what is the object of this questioning? *How did it come to this?* How could the people have fallen so far? The people who had something that no other nation had, *the assurance of favour from the King of the Universe*. Yet these people looked elsewhere:

> *"She weeps copiously in the night and her tears are on her cheeks. Among all her lovers she has no one to comfort her. All her friends have dealt treacherously with her, they have become her enemies."*
> (Lamentations 1:2)

These *lovers* would be the nations that Judah tried to ally itself with, such as Egypt and Assyria. Jeremiah spells it out:

> *"Judah has gone into captivity because of affliction and because of great*

servitude, dwelling among the nations she finds no rest. All her persecutors overtook her between the straits."
(Lamentations 1:3)

And the golden city of Jerusalem has been brought low:

"Jerusalem has grievously sinned, therefore she has become an abomination. All who honored her despise her because they have seen her nakedness: yea, she sighs and turns backward. Her filthiness is in her skirts, not remembering her last end. Therefore she came down amazingly, she had no comforter. LORD, behold my affliction, for the enemy has magnified himself."
(Lamentations 1:8–9)

The Temple in Jerusalem fell on the 9th day of Av, a recurring "9–11" for the Jewish people throughout their history. It was also on this day that the Second Temple would fall, at the hands of the Romans. Other tragedies stretch from the massacre in 132 AD, to the expulsion of the Jews from Britain and from Spain. On this annual "holiday", *Tisha B'Av*, it is the *Book of Lamentations* that is read in the synagogues.

The city suffered awfully at the hands of the Babylonians. Chapter four is graphic in its descriptions of the slaughter, of the thirst and hunger, the withered emaciated bodies, mothers eating their own children. It must have been so hard for Jeremiah to see these awful fulfilments.

"My eyes fail with tears, my insides are troubled, my liver is poured upon the earth for the destruction of the daughter of my people, because the children and those nursing swoon in the streets of the city."
(Lamentations 2:11)

God is silent but Jeremiah offers one last plea, with the anguished heart he shared with all of God's true prophets through the ages:

*"You, L*ORD*, remain forever; Your throne from generation to generation.*
*Why do You forget us forever, forsake us for so long? Turn us to You, L*ORD*,*
and we will be turned. Renew our days as of old. For will You utterly
reject us, be very angry against us?"
(Lamentations 5:19–22)

Surely Christians today have a responsibility not just to help
the Jewish people turn back to their LORD, but never again to
be responsible for any more *Tisha B'Avs?*

The Song of Songs

Do you remember the familiar scenario in the old Benny Hill
shows? To the catchy tune that has now unwelcomingly
appeared in your memory, Benny would weave in and around
a bevy of beauties, who would all usually manage to stay
beyond his grasp. Well, strike out Benny and replace him with
King Solomon. He with his 700 wives and 300 concubines. You
could imagine the comedy moments when Solomon visits a
harem that must have been the size of a small town and endeavours to perform his conjugal (and extra-marital) duties. An
awful lot of wanderings and snatched moments I would
imagine. Followed by exhaustion!

What has this to do with the *Song of Songs?* Well, Solomon
was said to be the probable author and, if the content of this
short book is to be taken literally, then he must have been at
the height of his virility as the book seems to be a rather erotic
love poem. Not everyone agrees with this, in fact some even
doubt Solomon as author. Is it about the love between a man
and a woman or is it an *allegory* of something deeper?

Well, I have been set a challenge. To be frank, for the first few
times I read The Song of Songs, it made little sense to me. Who
are doing the talking? Who are they talking about? Is it a man,
is it a woman? Not a good start, particularly as the challenge is
to make this a memorable section of my book. So, here goes . . .

Firstly, its title suggests that it's the song *above all songs*. As we don't know the tune, then the lyrics are going to have to be something very special; perhaps they are going to transport us to new places where we are to glimpse God in fresh ways.

My initial difficulty was in determining whose voice we are hearing. The NIV offers help by labelling the sections, converting it into a drama script. But, as with all additions, this was *not* in the original Hebrew as God intended and so may even hinder our reading of it.

So what is it? A love poem? An allegory of God's love for Israel, or for the Church? We need to know, as this is God's song *above all songs*, the greatest song ever. What would be the point of it if no-one could agree what it's all about? Mind you, does anyone know what *A Whiter shade of Pale* is all about, though Procol Harum had hallucinogenic drugs as their excuse!

Well, the *Hebraic Mind* allows us to pontificate, to accept that God can intend multiple levels of meaning, depending on our particular needs as we read His Word. So, perhaps we can just accept that all of the above understandings are applicable at any given moment.

Or, perhaps, there's more. Perhaps – and this is just a thought – God wants us to focus on the act and not the subject. Perhaps it is just a book about *love*, in all of its hues and flavours, from the erotic to the divine? Perhaps we should not focus on circumstance or identity, but rather on the God-given process of two hearts becoming as one and the longing that ensues when they are separated.

Perhaps, in His wisdom, He allows us to consider this book as either a celebration of marriage, or an assurance of His love for His physical and His spiritual people, but that His real intention is to teach us how to love each other?

Perhaps that's why it's the greatest song ever, because each of us can truly own it and learn something of this amazing, mysterious process that connects us all together . . . *this crazy little thing called love.*

The Book of Ecclesiastes

A favourite trick of the cynics is to challenge Bible believers to declare the infallibility of the Bible then hit them with a passage from Ecclesiastes, such as, *for that which befalls the sons of men befalls beasts . . . so that a man has no pre-eminence above a beast, for all is vanity* (Ecclesiastes 3:19).

Aha! They cry, *it's in the Bible, so it must be true!* Yes, it's in the Bible, but as the honest words of a defeated, depressed man, who had everything and threw it away. It is a man pouring himself out into the pages, warts and all, left in God's word as a lesson for us to heed.

Ecclesiastes is a book that fails to mention the LORD once by His name because it has been written by a man who has lost his intimacy with his Creator. Any mention of God is in the third person and it is His generic name, *Elohim*, that is used. There is no mention of repentance, atonement or the need to return to God. Does it have any redeeming features? What can we learn from it? Who is this man?

The man is King Solomon, at one time the richest and wisest man on the Earth. *Oh how the mighty have fallen!* The man who had it all reduced to a bitter husk, suffused with defeatism, pessimism, stoicism and memories of a hedonistic life, who had utterly betrayed the destiny that God had laid out for him with a warning:

> *"But if you will at all turn from following Me, you or your children, and will not keep My commandments and My statutes which I have set before you, but go and serve other gods and worship them, then I will cut off Israel from the land which I have given them, and this House, which I have sanctified for My name, I shall cast out of My sight and Israel will be a proverb and a byword among all people."*
> (1 Kings 9:6–7)

As we have already seen, Solomon heeded this not, took on a massive harem of pagan ladies and *served other gods*. For this he (or rather his son) lost his Kingdom and, as we see in Ecclesiastes, lost far more.

His persistent refrain was, *all is vanity and a striving after wind.* Everything is temporary, ungraspable, pointless. There's a lot of self-pity here and we begin to wonder what we can actually learn from this broken man. Well, there are still fragments of the great wisdom that God had once bestowed on him.

> *"The thing that has been, it is that which will be, and that which is done is that which will be done and there is no new thing under the sun. Is there anything of which it may be said, See, this is new? It has been already from olden times, which were before us."*
> (Ecclesiastes 1:9–10)

There is no new thing under the sun. How true is that!? What this says to us is that what happened 2000, 3000 or more years ago is still totally relevant to us today. And the reason for this is that our minds may have developed in cleverness, thanks to the relentless deluge of new information that has been fed in from the world over the centuries, *but the souls of mankind are just as wicked as they have ever been!* There is no new thing under the sun. We can learn from Solomon in Ecclesiastes, we can learn from both the mistakes and triumphs of Abraham, of Moses, of David and others. The Bible is as relevant today as it was the day it ever was. And, of course, God never changes.

Rather than pick apart the words of this sorry man, let's jump to his own conclusions at the end of the book:

> *"Let us hear the conclusion of the whole matter: Revere God and keep His commandments: for this is the whole man. For God will bring every work into judgment, concerning every hidden thing, whether it is good, or whether it is evil."*
> (Ecclesiastes 12:13–14)

Not spoken with any passion, but with weary acknowledgement. Let us be careful that we too don't lose what we
once had.

The Book of Habakkuk

Here's someone we know virtually nothing about, except that
he lived at about the same time as Jeremiah, probably witnessed
the Babylonian sacking of Jerusalem and was possibly a Levite
or even a singer in the Temple.

Habakkuk had some spark in him as he twice challenges God
on some pretty deep stuff. This was no *Our Father Abraham*
(Avraham Avinu) or *Our Rabbi Moses* (Moshe Rabbeinu) speaking
with the One who regularly spoke to them. This was perhaps a
Jerusalem chorister, certainly no-one special in the grand scheme
of things, by our way of thinking. We don't even know who his
father was. Yet this man dared to ask God *why He was doing
nothing about the wickedness in the land*, then, when God declared
that, *don't worry the Babylonians are coming*, dared to challenge
Him on his choice of chastisers:

> "*Therefore why do You look upon those who deal treacherously and hold
> Your tongue when the wicked devours the man that is more righteous
> than he?*"
> (Habakkuk 1:13)

God replies, *don't worry, trust Me. The Babylonians will get
what's due to them also!* He does this with a series of generic
proverbs that, though directed in this case at the Babylonians,
would serve well as a warning to all future tyrants.

> "*Woe to him who increases that which is not his! How long? And woe
> to him who loads himself with pledges. Will they not rise up suddenly
> who will bite you and awake who will vex you and you will be for looting
> to them? Because you have plundered many nations, all the remnant of*

*the peoples will plunder you, because of men's blood and for the violence
of the land, of the city, and of all who live there."*
(Habakkuk 2:6–8)

We live in uncertain times. It is more uncertain than most
think because the majority of the world (and some in the
Church) don't see that, just like in the final days of Judah, we
too are ripe for judgement. It may surprise us, too, *who* God
uses as our chastisers.

Instead of reacting in haste to the secularisers without and
the liberalisers within, we should opt for the *preventative* remedy
of getting our act together so that God doesn't need to send us
chastisers. Occasionally we have to burst out of our Christian
bubbles and find out what's on God's agenda, rather than
reacting to the world's agenda. That should be our focus.

The important thing is to look beyond the immediate and
get clear in our minds *just Who is pulling the strings* and look
beyond the chastisers and consider the One who sent them.

And then we must get on our knees . . .

The Book of Ezekiel

Here's a man who really suffered for his labours. From eating
scrolls, to living a visibly nomadic life, to losing his wife, he had
to act out his role as a prophetic sign to Israel. It all started with
the first of many amazing visions, as he languished by the River
of Babylon, as one of the earliest exiles from Judah. God spoke
to him, after appearing to him in His Glory:

*"And He said to me, Son of man, stand upon your feet and I shall speak
to you. And the Spirit entered me when He spoke to me and set me upon
my feet, so I heard Him Who spoke to me. And He said to me, Son of
man, I am sending you to the children of Israel, to a rebellious nation
that has rebelled against Me. They and their fathers have transgressed
against Me, to this very day. For they are impudent children and stiff*

hearted. *I am sending you to them and you will say to them, the word of Adonai, the* LORD. *And they, whether they will hear, or whether they will hold back, (for they are a rebellious house) will yet know that there has been a prophet among them."*
(Ezekiel 2:1–5)

There are two incidental points of interest here. God calls Ezekiel *Son of man*. This is not to be confused with Jesus' title, which is taken from a supernatural vision in the Book of Daniel. Ezekiel is just an ordinary man, though he was an ordained priest and his title is akin to the description of the Pevensey children in the Narnia books, as *sons of Adam* and *daughters of Eve*. Ezekiel is just a representative of the human race.

The other interesting observation here is that Ezekiel is sent to the children of *Israel*. Yet we are told that most of Israel, the Northern Kingdom, was sent into exile years earlier by the Assyrians. It is clear that the terms Judah and Israel are now interchangeable, in fact Ezekiel, when speaking of Judah, actually uses the term *Israel* far more than *Judah*!

Although Ezekiel is in exile, the city of Jerusalem has not yet been captured and so much of his prophecy is a warning of the impending judgement, a theme we have already seen with other prophets, such as Jeremiah and Habbakuk.

"Thus says Adonai, the LORD, *This is Jerusalem. I have set it in the midst of the nations and countries that are all around her. And she rebelled against My judgments more wickedly than the nations and against My statutes more than the countries that are around her, for they have refused My judgments and My statutes, they have not walked in them. Therefore thus says Adonai, the* LORD, *Because you are turbulent more than the nations who are around you and have not walked in My statutes, neither have you kept My judgments nor have you done according to the judgments of the nations that are around you. Therefore thus says Adonai, the* LORD, *Behold! I, even I* AM *against you and will execute justice in your midst in the sight of the nations. And I shall do in you that which*

I have not done and which I shall not do any more like it because of all
your abominations. "
(Ezekiel 5:5–9)

So how bad had things got in the city that was once Jerusalem
the Golden, capital city of David and Solomon? Bad enough!
Judgement was deserved, it seems. Here are some low points:

"The city sheds blood in its midst so that her time will come and she makes
idols against herself to defile herself. . . . Behold the princes of Israel, each
was in you for his power to shed blood. They have lightly esteemed father
and mother within you. In your midst they have dealt by oppression with
the stranger. Within you they have vexed the fatherless and the widow.
You have despised My holy things and have violated My Sabbaths. Among
you are men who carry tales to shed blood, and in your midst they eat
upon the mountains. In your midst they commit lewdness. In you they
have discovered their fathers' nakedness. Among you they have humbled
her who was set apart for pollution. And one has committed abomination
with his neighbor's wife and another has lewdly defiled his daughter-in-
law and another in you has humbled his sister, his father's daughter. In
you they have taken bribes to shed blood. You have taken usury and interest
and you have greedily gained from your neighbors by extortion and have
forgotten Me: the word of Adonai, the Lord. "
(Ezekiel 22:3, 6–12)

Probably much the same that goes on in a typical city in
today's world. Frightening thought, isn't it, when you consider
the penalty *Jerusalem* had to pay? Yet God is the same yesterday,
today and forever!
Judgement finally came for them, the Babylonians.

"For I am *the* Lord! *I shall speak and the word that I speak will come to*
pass. It will no longer be delayed, for in your days, O rebellious house, I
will say the word and will perform it: the word of Adonai, the Lord. "
(Ezekiel 12:25)

Once Ezekiel has made clear this message of judgement, small glimmers of hope begin to appear, promises of a future return from exile. Here's one of the first mentions:

> *"And I shall bring you out from the peoples and will gather you out of the countries where you are scattered with a mighty hand and with an outstretched arm and with fury poured out."*
> (Ezekiel 20:34)

He then declares the contempt God has for those nations who came against His people, with their pagan ideas and violent ways. Ammon, Moab, Seir, Edom, Philistia, Tyre and Sidon all get both barrels! Then Ezekiel rails against Egypt and Elam and, again, nestled among these stark judgements is comfort for His people, as if to say, *I am willing to forget these other nations, but I will never abandon you.*

> *"Thus says Adonai, the* LORD, *when I have gathered the House of Israel from the peoples among whom they are scattered and I am sanctified in them in the sight of the nations, then they will live in their land that I have given to My servant Jacob. And they will dwell safely there and build houses and plant vineyards. Yes, they will dwell with confidence when I have executed judgments upon all those around them who despise them, and they will know that I* AM *the* LORD *their God."*
> (Ezekiel 28:25–26)

And there's a reason for this, one that is either missed or neglected. Either way, there's a possibility of many Christians today **making a major error in their understanding of their God**.

> *"Therefore say to the House of Israel, Thus says Adonai, the* LORD, *I* AM *not doing this for your sake, O House of Israel, but for My holy name's sake, which you have profaned among the nations wherever you went. And I shall sanctify My great name, which was profaned among the nations, which you have profaned in their midst, and the nations will*

know that I AM the LORD, says Adonai, the LORD, when I am sanctified
in you before their eyes."
(Ezekiel 36:22–23)

So what is God doing for *His holy Name's sake*? What is He
going to do that will draw all to Him? What mighty wonders
will He perform that will raise a banner among the nations?
This is going to be something awesome indeed and surely
no-one will miss it. What is it, then? Well, let's read the next
few verses, familiar to some:

> *"For I shall take you from among the nations and gather you out of all*
> *the countries and will bring you into your own land. Then I shall sprinkle*
> *clean water upon you and you will be clean from all your filthiness and*
> *from all your idols. I shall cleanse you. And I will give you a new heart*
> *and I will put a new Spirit within you and I will take away the stony*
> *heart from your flesh and I will give you a heart of flesh. And I shall put*
> *My Spirit within you and cause you to walk in My statutes and you will*
> *keep and do My judgments. And you will dwell in the land that I gave to*
> *your fathers and you will be My people and I AM will be your God."*
> (Ezekiel 36:24–28)

So, let's get this right. *For His holy Name's sake*, God is going
to return Israel to their land, in order to eventually turn them
back to Him. So, if we miss this, *then we are missing a self-declared*
act of God, for His holy Name's sake.

Those Christians who miss this fact, either through ignorance
or prejudice, who can't admit that the birth of modern Israel
is not just history but *His Story*, are **denying the One they claim**
to serve. This is serious.

Ezekiel was a watchman, an observer and interpreter of
what he saw around him.

> *"So you, O son of man, I have set you as a watchman for the House of*
> *Israel. Therefore you will hear the word at My mouth and warn them*

from Me. When I say to the wicked, O wicked man, you will surely die,
if you do not speak to warn the wicked from his way, that wicked man
will die in his iniquity, but I shall require his blood at your hand.
Nevertheless, if you warn the wicked to turn from his way: if he does
not turn from his way, he will die in his iniquity, but you have delivered
your life."
(Ezekiel 33:7–9)

If we consider ourselves watchmen, we must realise what a
serious responsibility we have taken on. We need to be willing
to speak truth, whatever the consequences to ourselves and to
others. This is hard and it's only going to get harder in our
world of political (and spiritual) correctness.

What about those of us called to other positions? What
about those pastors among us?

"And the word of the LORD came to me saying, Son of man, prophesy
against the shepherds of Israel. Prophesy and say to them, thus says
Adonai, the LORD to the shepherds, Woe to the shepherds of Israel who
feed themselves! Should not the shepherds feed the flocks? You eat the fat
and you clothe yourself with the wool, you kill those that are fed, but
you do not feed the flock."
(Ezekiel 34:1–3)

A pastor is a shepherd of people (it's the same word in
Hebrew). Are you giving more than you take, are you feeding
your flock, or *feeding from them?* Be very careful, because there
is a judgement for those who misuse their position:

"Therefore, you shepherds, Listen! Obey the word of the LORD! As I AM
living, says Adonai, the LORD, surely because My flock became a prey and
My flock became food for every beast of the field because there was no
shepherd, nor did My shepherds search for My flock, but the shepherds
fed themselves and did not feed My flock, therefore, O you shepherds,
Listen! Obey the word of the LORD. Thus says Adonai, the LORD, Behold,

I am against the shepherds and I shall require My flock at their hand,
and cause them to cease from feeding the flock. Neither will the shepherds
feed themselves any more, for I shall deliver My flock from their mouth,
so they will not be food for them."
(Ezekiel 34:7–10)

I am not singling out pastors for such a negative treatment,
I'm simply making a point about our approach to Old Testament prophecy. We tend to spiritualise and claim the positive
prophecies for our own use, because they edify, enrich or
empower us. But the negative ones (of which there are far
more) we prefer to leave in their original context . . . for the
people of Israel at that time. We must be consistent in our use of
Scripture and particularly the Book of Ezekiel, because it's full
of such examples, such as the *Dry Bones* (Ezekiel 37:1–9), the
Two Sticks (Ezekiel 37:15–28), *Gog and Magog* (Ezekiel 38)
and the controversial and confusing *Third Temple* (Ezekiel 40
onwards).

He finishes his book with a single statement, a Name for God
that appears nowhere else: *The* Lord *is There (YHWH Shammah).*
It refers to the future city of Jerusalem (Yerushalayim) and can
even be a Hebrew word-play, embedding God's title within the
actual name of the city.

Is God's Name embedded within our hearts? Now there's a
question! And, above all, in all that we do, do we always act *for*
the sake of His holy Name?

By the River

The Book of Daniel

What a book! It's such a good read in its own right, whether you are a Christian or not. But it's much more than that. It is so God-affirming, full of derring-do and righteous exploits, it must *surely* be one of God's favourite books too.

So who was Daniel? First let's consider *Nebuchadnezzar*, the King of Babylon who invaded Judah. His name has become a bit of a mouthful, so I'm going to call him *Nebbish*, a Yiddish word, meaning "submissive". This will make sense later on.

Anyway, Daniel was one of the talented, favoured young men who ended up in Nebbish's palace, to learn the ways of the Babylonians. He immediately made a mark in his stand against the palace food, refusing to defile his body in accordance with the Torah and was granted a vegetarian diet, once he proved that it wouldn't be detrimental to his health. Daniel had three friends, best known by the Babylonian names of *Shadrach*, *Meshach* and *Abednego*. Daniel 1:17 says, *"As for these four boys, God gave them knowledge and skill in all learning and wisdom and Daniel had understanding in all visions and dreams."*

Now, in the Jewish Bible (Tenach), the Book of Daniel is included among the *writings* (ketuvim) rather than the *prophets* (nevi'im). Was Daniel not a prophet? How strange. This is worth examining. Although Daniel was considered a prophet in early versions of the *Talmud, Rashi,* a highly influential 11th Century Jewish scholar, disagreed and had him replaced. His stated reason was that, to be qualified as a prophet, one needs to cater to the needs of people living in his time. As Daniel's prophecies were for the future, then this disqualified him, in Rashi's view. In his commentary on the Talmud, Rashi accepts that Daniel was a prophet, but not one sent with a prophetic message for his people, in his day.

Yet even to this untrained mind, something nags at me. Daniel was very much a man of his day and although interpretations were for the future, he also spoke to the people of his day. And, despite the fact that his prophecies were for the future and not for the present, *prophecies* they still were. No greater authority than Jesus himself confirms the standing of Daniel. In Matthew 24:15 he calls him "... *the prophet Daniel* ..." But, of course, Rashi and the rabbis don't share in our confidence in Jesus as the final word.

Perhaps there was a personal reason for this because, in Daniel 9, we have perhaps the most telling of all prophecies for the coming of the Messiah, the one that fairly accurately forecasts the date of this momentous event:

> *"Know therefore and understand, that from the going forth of the commandment to restore and to build Jerusalem until the Messiah Prince will be seven weeks: and during sixty-two weeks it will be built again, with street and trench, even in troubled times. And after sixty-two weeks the Messiah will be cut off and there will be no one to succeed Him,"*
> (Daniel 9:25–26)

If you are intrigued there's a more detailed discussion on this in my book, *Jesus, Man of Many Names* ...

You get the sense, when you read this chapter, of a steady build up to this key prophecy. Daniel, noticing that the seventy-year exile predicted by Jeremiah was reaching its latter stages, felt a responsibility to ... *do a Jeremiah.*

"And I set my face toward the Lord God, to seek by prayer and suppli-
cations with fasting and sackcloth and ashes. And I prayed to the Lord
my God and made my confession and said, My Lord, Great and Awesome
God, keeping the covenant and loving kindness for those who love Him
and for those who keep His commandments, We have sinned and have
committed iniquity and have done wickedly and have rebelled, even by
departing from Your commands and from Your judgments."
(Daniel 9:3–5)

It carries on in this vein and culminates with an appearance
of the angel Gabriel, who *always* has something significant to
say. He did. It was the prophecy of Daniel 9:25, predicting when
the Messiah was to come, something that he was going to have
a hand in at the fulfilment, when he was going to appear again
to young *Miriam* (Mary) and her betrothed, *Yosef* (Joseph), in
the village of Nazareth.

Back to Nebbish. He had a troubling dream, which he
promptly forgot on waking and could find no-one to tell him
what he dreamt and then interpret it. Only Daniel was able to
do this and we reveal how:

"Then the secret was revealed to Daniel in a night vision and Daniel blessed
the God of Heaven. Daniel answered and said, blessed be the name of God
forever and ever, for wisdom and might are His, and He changes the times
and the seasons. He removes kings and sets up kings. He gives wisdom to the
wise and knowledge to those who know understanding. He reveals the deep
and secret things, He knows what is in the darkness, and the light dwells
with Him. I thank you and praise You, O You God of my fathers, Who has
given me wisdom and might and has made known to me now what we
desired of You, for You have now made known to us the king's matter."
(Daniel 2:19–23)

What a passage! Daniel is revealing the Source of all wisdom
and he worshipped Him. This is to set the tone for the whole
book and it's not just Daniel who *carries the baton.* Nebbish

himself is amazed at Daniel's dream interpretation and said, *it is of a truth that your God is a God of gods, and a Lord of kings, and a Revealer of Secrets, seeing you could reveal this secret* (Daniel 2:47). But this didn't stop Nebbish from erecting a hundred foot tower of himself for his people to forcibly worship! If they refused, then it was the burning fiery furnace for them! Shadrach, Meshach and Abednego refused, saying:

> *"Behold, our God Whom we serve is able to deliver us from the burning fiery furnace and He will deliver us out of your hand, O king. But if not, be it known to you, O king, that we will not serve your gods or worship the golden image which you have set up."*
> (Daniel 3:17–18)

These three brave men were setting themselves up as the first recorded Jewish martyrs, though they were sure that God would rescue them. He did, of course. Nebbish again surprises us:

> *"Blessed be the God of Shadrach, Meshach, and Abednego, Who has sent His angel and delivered His servants who trusted in Him and have changed the king's word and yielded their bodies, so they could not serve or worship any god except their own God. Therefore I make a decree, that every people, nation, and language that speaks anything amiss against the God of Shadrach, Meshach, and Abednego, will be cut in pieces and their houses will be made a dunghill because there is no other God that can deliver after this sort."*
> (Daniel 3:28–29)

He then had another dream and again Daniel interpreted it. But it wasn't a good one for Nebbish:

> *"This is the interpretation, O king, and this is the decree of the Most High, which has come upon my lord the king so they will drive you from men and your dwelling will be with the beasts of the field, and they will make you to eat grass like oxen and they will wet you with the dew of*

heaven, and seven times will pass over you, until you know that the Most High rules in the kingdom of men, and gives it to whomever He will. "
(Daniel 4:21–22 – this is Daniel 4:24–25 in other versions)

So *Nebuchadnezzar*, the great ruler of the known world becomes a true "nebbish" and is reduced to eating grass until he wholeheartedly acknowledges Who was The True King:

"And at the end of the days I Nebuchadnezzar lifted up my eyes to heaven, and my understanding returned to me and I blessed the Most High and I praised and honored Him Who Lives Forever, Whose dominion is an everlasting dominion, and His kingdom is from generation to generation. "
(Daniel 4:31 – this is Daniel 4:34 in other versions)

Nebbish has an about turn! This is equivalent to Hitler or Stalin getting a reprieve from God for all their evil acts. It's just beyond our comprehension how deep and unfathomable is the grace and mercy of the Lord. No one is beyond redemption, despite our unwillingness to contemplate this.

Yet we are not to judge. It is not for us to challenge His decisions; it has been the downfall of many a Christian throughout time. We must let God . . . be God.

The Book of Haggai

Around a year after Gabriel had given that momentous prophecy to Daniel, God sent Haggai to *Zerubbabel*, the governor of the exiles and to the high priest.

"Thus says the LORD of Hosts saying, this people says, the time has not come, the time that the LORD's House should be built. "
(Haggai 1:2)

It was time for the exiled people from Judah – the Jews – to repair God's house. Darius, the Persian king, was up for it, it

was the Jews who weren't so keen. But Haggai was to stir them
up on this issue.

> *"Is it time for you, O you, to live in your roofed houses, while this House*
> *is waste? Now therefore thus says the* Lord *of Hosts, Consider your ways.*
> *You have sown much, and brought in little. You eat, but you do not have*
> *enough. You drink, but you are not filled with drink. You clothe yourself,*
> *but no one is warm, and he who earns wages earns wages to put in a bag*
> *with holes."*
> (Haggai 1:4–6)

He prompts them to consider why things aren't working out
too well for them. Never enough to eat or drink, never warm
enough. *Could this not be from God? Of course it was! Then, listen*
to what I'm telling you then!

How many Christians today are happy to take part in huge
worship events and nationwide prayer initiatives, but are purposefully blind to God *actually working* in the world. There's a
whiff here of that old peculiarly British heresy, *Deism*, which has
a view of God as a kindly (or a stern) old man in the sky who
got things started but doesn't do much else. When a Christian
politician in 2014 blamed recent extraordinary weather patterns
on God's displeasure at the legalising of gay marriage, he was
vilified and laughed at by most Christians. Why, as they seem
to be saying, is God silent now at the blatant disregard of His
laws, when He was so assertive in Bible times? Is He still interested in us? *More than we are in Him, it seems!*

> *"Then Zerubbabel the son of Shaltiel and Joshua the son of Jehozadak*
> *the high priest, with the entire remnant of the people, obeyed the voice*
> *of the* Lord *their God,"*
> (Haggai 1:12)

They all listened! Now there's a first! So Haggai reminded
them what the Temple used to mean to them.

*"Who is left among you who saw this House in its first glory? And
how do you see it now? Is it not as nothing in your eyes in com-
parison to it? Yet now strengthen, O Zerubbabel! Says the* LORD,
*Strengthen, O Joshua, son of Jehozadak the high priest! Strengthen all
you people of the land! says the* LORD. *Work! For I* AM *with you, says
the* LORD *of Hosts."*
(Haggai 2:3–4)

And so they did. Zerubbabel took his God seriously and, in
return, was mentioned in dispatches:

"In that day, says the LORD *of Hosts, I shall take you, O Zerubbabel, My
servant, the son of Shaltiel, says the* LORD, *and will make you like a
signet, for I have chosen you, says the* LORD *of Hosts."*
(Haggai 2:23)

What does this mean? In which day? How was he chosen?
Signet rings were used by Kings as a symbol of their power and
authority. So what was special about Zerubbabel? Well, he's the
only royal personage after King David who is mentioned in
both of Jesus' family lines (Matthew 1 and Luke 3). He was
therefore chosen, as was David, to be part of the *Messianic line*,
the most glorious family-line of all. What a privilege!

This man listened to the words of the prophet and acted
accordingly and correctly. For that reason, his name was
cemented into the greatest genealogical line of all, remembered
for all time. What a legacy!

Will we leave behind a legacy as someone who has listened
to the Word of God?

The Book of Zechariah

God was speaking to Zechariah about the same time as Haggai.
But He had a lot more to say to Zechariah and, through him,
to his people . . . and ultimately to us.

The book opens with a call to repentance, a plea for the Jews to break free from the cycle of sin and consequences that had trapped them again and again in the past. God speaks as the LORD of Hosts, which adds impact to the words:

"The LORD has been greatly displeased with your fathers. Therefore say to them, Thus says the LORD of Hosts, Return yourselves to Me! says the LORD of Hosts! Then I shall turn to you, says the LORD of Hosts."
(Zechariah 1:2–3)

Zechariah is then given a series of eight visions, each with an explanation, some relevant to his generation, others speaking of future times. The first one is worth noting, as it dovetails nicely with the prophecy of Haggai. We eavesdrop on a heavenly conversation and are privy to God's declaration:

"Therefore thus says the LORD, I have returned to Jerusalem with com-passion. My House will be built in it, says the LORD of Hosts, and a line will be stretched forth over Jerusalem."
(Zechariah 1:16)

The rest of the book tends to focus on three areas, subjects of intense interest to modern Christians and therefore sufficient reason to make this prophetic book a favourite for many who like to speculate on things that are still to come.

Two of these areas are *Jerusalem* and *the End Times*, very much seen together in some very evocative passages:

"Thus says the LORD, I have returned to Zion and will dwell in the midst of Jerusalem and Jerusalem will be called The City of Truth and the mountain of the LORD of Hosts, The Holy Mountain."
(Zechariah 8:3)

"Behold, I AM will make Jerusalem a cup of trembling for all the peoples round about, when they and Judah will be in the siege against Jerusalem.

And in that Day I shall make Jerusalem a burdensome stone for all the peoples. All who burden themselves with it will be severely injured, though all the peoples of the earth are gathered together against it."
(Zechariah 12:2–3)

"And it will be in that Day, I shall seek to destroy all the nations that come against Jerusalem."
(Zechariah 12:9)

With the most evocative of all:

"Behold, the Day of the Lord *is coming and booty from you will be divided in your presence. For I shall gather all the nations against Jerusalem in battle and the city will be taken and the houses rifled and the women ravished, and half the city will go into captivity and the rest of the people will not be cut off from the city. Then the* Lord *will go forth and fight against those nations, like when He fought in the day of battle. And His feet will stand in that Day upon the Mount of Olives, which is before Jerusalem on the east, and the Mount of Olives will split in the middle toward the east and toward the west and there will be a very great valley, and half of the mountain will remove toward the north and half of it toward the south. And you will flee to the valley of the mountains, for the valley of the mountains will reach to Azel. Yes, you will flee, like you fled from before the earthquake in the days of Uzziah king of Judah and the* Lord *my God will come and all the saints with you."*
(Zechariah 14:1–5)

What a story this tells. The detail of this story is explicit and a real problem for those who prefer to spiritualise Scripture and shy away from literal fulfilments, particularly when the script is not to their liking.

The story is inescapable because those with ears to hear can see the drama being acted out on the world's stage. Jerusalem is not just central to God's purpose, as the Scripture shows us, but this tiny city in this pariah nation is, without a shadow of a doubt, *central to the world's agenda*. The idea that this prophet, countless centuries ago, predicted that a time would come when it would be *a burdensome stone for all the peoples*, is unbelievable *(in fact, most don't believe it!)*.

This is incontestable. Jerusalem (and, by implication, the Nation of Israel) has been condemned by more United Nation resolutions then every other world city combined! No nation recognises its status as the capital city of Israel. No other city in the world has been such a provocation to the nations. It's *no wonder, really*. God has proven time and time again that He has even the enemies of His people in His hands, to do and think whatever He wants, in order to fulfil His purposes. This is on display but most people, even many Christians, fail to see this!

Christians need to wake up to this, because the Scripture is absolutely explicit as to what is going to happen to the nations that attack Jerusalem and how this will be the *very place* where Jesus Christ will return. Then what will happen afterwards? Scripture even makes this very clear:

> *"And it will be that everyone that is left of all the nations who came against Jerusalem will go up from year to year to worship the King, the* Lord *of Hosts, and to keep the Feast of Sukkot. And it will be that whoever will not come up of the families of the earth to Jerusalem to worship the King, the* Lord *of Hosts; even upon them there will be no rain."*
> (Zechariah 14:16–17)

Some of you may be wondering, Feast of Sukkot, what's this? *How are we going to keep that feast if we've never heard of it?* Well, it is a biblical feast, unlike Christmas, Easter or any other traditional festivals. You can read about it in Leviticus 23:33–36 and the reason why the Church has forgotten it, is that the Church has deliberately forgotten its *Hebraic roots*, in the same way as Stalinist Russia chose to forget those considered enemies of the State and airbrushed them from history, and even photographs. (For more on this, read my book, *How the Church Lost the Way.*)

Earlier I mentioned *one* other area that Zechariah touches on. This may surprise some of you. He says an awful lot about *Jesus.* We have already seen the Second Coming covered, in terms of his appearance in Jerusalem and his installation as true King of the world in that same place. But, also . . .

> *"Thus says the LORD of Hosts saying, Behold the Man whose name is The Branch (Sprout), and He will grow up out of His place and He will build the Palace of the LORD and He will bear the glory and will sit and rule upon His throne and He will be a priest upon His throne and the counsel of Shalom will be between them both."*
> (Zechariah 6:12–13)

> *"So they weighed for My price thirty pieces of silver. And the LORD said to me, Throw it to the treasury, a goodly price that I prized of them. And I took the thirty pieces of silver and threw them into the treasury in the House of the LORD."*
> (Zechariah 11:12–13)

> *"Awake, O sword, against My shepherd and against My fellow man, says the LORD of Hosts. Strike the shepherd and the sheep will be scattered and I shall turn My hand against the little ones."*
> (Zechariah 13:7)

> *"Rejoice very exuberantly, O daughter of Zion! Shout, O daughter of Jerusalem! Behold, your King will come to you. He is just and having victory, lowly and riding on a donkey, even on a colt, the foal of a donkey. And I will cut off the chariot from Ephraim and the horse from Jerusalem and the battle bow will be cut off, and He will speak Shalom to the nations. And His dominion will be from sea to sea and from the River Euphrates to the ends of the earth."*
> (Zechariah 9:9–10)

"And the LORD *will be King over all the earth. In that Day the* LORD *will be One and His name One."*
(Zechariah 14:9)

Many Christians these days consider themselves *People of the Book*, but, rather than speaking of the whole Bible, they call themselves *New Testament* Christians. By doing so they deprive themselves of a true understanding of their God. What they are exhibiting is a symptom of our age of *consumerism*, a desire for results and experiences, without an understanding of the source. There's a danger that a high proportion of Christians in our society are so ignorant of the foundations of our faith, that it will take just the slightest breeze of persecution or uncertainty to blow the faith right out of them!

Why do we need the Old Testament? If you have ever asked this question, *hopefully you are not asking it anymore!*

The Book of Esther

"For such a time as this."

How many conferences, gatherings, convocations and assemblies have you seen with this very title? Torn screaming and shouting from its contextual root in the pages of the book of Esther, what do these events really have in common with the brave act of a simple Jewess, elevated to royal favour thanks to her comeliness and in a position to save her people from extinction?

And that, in a nutshell, is the book of *Esther*. She lived as a Jewish exile, now in the Persian empire, which had supplanted the Babylonian one, in the reign of King Ahasuerus. Her story is the foundation for the Jewish feast of *Purim*, a joyous occasion celebrating the triumph of good over evil. You can download a free comedy drama I wrote for the event at http://www.hebrewroots.com/node/135.

But where was God? It's the only book in the Hebrew Scriptures that does *not* mention His name even once. Isn't that strange?

Not a *single* mention! It's almost as if the Bible tells us that if the writer has purposely done so, to make a point. And, if so, what is this point? Perhaps the author is encouraging us to *read between the lines* for the divine? So, if He's not there explicitly, then where *do* we find Him in those pages?

First we see the character of the main protagonists. There was Mordechai's willingness to adopt his cousin Esther and look after her as a father. Then there was Esther's purity, perhaps this was what attracted the King to her, as a contrast from the rest of his harem? In fact we read:

"... *And Esther obtained favor in the sight of all those who looked upon her.*"
(Esther 2:15)

We also read that she continued to follow Mordechai's instructions and to live as a daughter of the commandments, even as a soul separated from the bosom of her own community.

Then there was Mordechai and his unwillingness to bow in homage to the evil Haman, as no true Jew would. This brought terrible consequences:

"... *therefore Haman sought to destroy all the Jews, the people of Mordecai that were throughout the whole kingdom of Ahasuerus.*"
(Esther 3:6)

Haman declares that the Jews are different from all other people and that they alone did not follow the King's laws. That was because the Jews had laws of their own, *the Torah.*

When the proclamation goes out that the Jews are to be destroyed because of this, the Jews in the land are given a choice. If they relent and agree to abide by the King's laws then surely the decree would be withdrawn. Instead we see them not budging in their devotion to God and willing to bear the consequences:

"And in every province, wherever the king's commandment and his decree came, there was great mourning among the Jews, and fasting and weeping and wailing and many lay in sackcloth and ashes."
(Esther 4:3)

Then comes Mordechai's big speech to Esther:

"For if you altogether hold your peace at this time, then enlargement and deliverance will arise for the Jews from another place, but you and your father's house will be destroyed and who knows whether you have come to the kingdom for such a time as this?"
(Esther 4:14)

Mordechai is certain that his God will not abandon them and, if not through Esther, then through some other means. And what was Esther's response to this? That all should fast, in acknowledgement of their need for God's help, then she would approach the king, to petition him for the life of her people.

That night God acted and caused the King to discover how Mordechai had once saved his life. For this he decided to honour him and gave Haman the duty of doing so! That night Haman's wife gave him more bad news:

". . . If Mordecai is of the seed of the Jews, before whom you have begun to fall, you will not prevail against him, but will surely fall before him."
(Esther 6:13)

She knew that the Jews were a *chosen people*, whose enemies tended to come to a sticky end! As did Haman, the following day, on the gallows he had erected for Mordechai.

So the Jews were saved, not in the usual manner, through a great military victory, but through the actions of two ordinary Jews. Just as battles were only won when God was with them, so it was here too. God may not have been mentioned in this book, but He was very much present in the actions of Mordechai and Esther.

In the same way, we Christians must demonstrate God in *The Way* that we conduct ourselves, not just in our words and great proclamations.

And, as for Esther . . . this is not the end of her story.

The boys are back

The Book of Ezra

Here was a man for his times, a priest (in fact a descendant of Aaron), a scribe and one who *had prepared his heart to seek the Torah of the LORD and to do it and to teach statutes and judgements in Israel* (Ezra 7:10). A man who is truly going to lead his people and set a good example.

Another good leader was a surprising one, King Cyrus of Persia, who 79 years earlier, issued this proclamation:

> *"Thus says Cyrus king of Persia, the LORD God of Heaven has given me all the kingdoms of the earth, and He has charged me to build a House for Him in Jerusalem, which is in Judah. Who is there among you of all His people? His God will be with him, and let him go up to Jerusalem, which is in Judah, and build the House of the LORD God of Israel. He is the God that is in Jerusalem. And whoever remains in any place where he sojourns, let the men of his place help him with silver and with gold and with goods and with beasts, besides the freewill offering for the House of God that is in Jerusalem."*
>
> (Ezra 1:2–4)

This was the same man who Isaiah spoke of *by name*, many decades earlier:

"I shall direct all his ways. He will build My city and he will let My captives go, not for price or reward, says the LORD of Hosts."
(Isaiah 45:13)

The fact that Isaiah mentioned Cyrus by name (Isaiah 45:1) is why liberal commentators and historians have insisted that there was more than one *Isaiah*, with one of them speaking *after* the event, as the idea of such an accurate prophecy is troubling to them.

So we have the pagan Cyrus who seemed to be more in tune with the God of the Jews than the Jews were themselves. And, as we already read in *Haggai*, Zerubbabel was despatched to Jerusalem to organise the rebuilding of the Temple.

Now, 79 years later, there's a new Persian King, *Artaxerxes*, son of Ahaseurus, and thought by many to be half-Jewish, on account of his mother . . . *Esther*. So, this remarkable lady was perhaps instrumental in what happened next. Because this King wrote Ezra a letter, in which he states, *And now: I make a decree, that all those of the people of Israel and of its priests and Levites in my realm, who are minded of their own free will to go up to Jerusalem, go with you. Since you are sent by the king and his seven counsellors to inquire concerning Judah and Jerusalem, according to the law of your God, which is in your hand and to carry the silver and gold, which the king and his counsellors have freely offered to the God of Israel, Whose habitation is in Jerusalem* (Ezra 7:13–15).

Ezra wasn't going to argue with this and prepared for the hazardous journey to Jerusalem. He declared *a fast* as a way of gaining God's favour (as did Esther, when she needed God to act to save her nation), so that they would be protected on this journey, without needing a consort from the King. After all they were taking many of the Temple treasures with them, vessels of silver and gold. God was with them, *and He delivered us from the hand of the enemy and of such as lay in wait by the way* (Ezra 8:31).

When he arrived in Jerusalem there was a shock waiting for him:

> *"The princes came to me saying, the people of Israel and the priests and the Levites have not separated themselves from the peoples of the lands, according to their abominations, of the Canaanites, the Hittites, the Perizzites, the Jebusites, the Ammonites, the Moabites, the Egyptians, and the Amorites. For they have taken of their daughters for themselves, and for their sons, so that the holy seed has mixed themselves with the peoples of those lands: yea, the hand of the princes and rulers has been chief in this unfaithfulness."*
> (Ezra 9:1–2)

Had they not learnt anything during their seventy year exile? Surely they were all familiar at least with Jeremiah's warnings and exhortations? And priests were among the guilty parties, how much worse could it get?

Ezra was so disturbed he literally tore his hair out and sat down for many hours, utterly appalled. He was joined by like-minded people, *those who trembled at the words of the God of Israel*, so at least he wasn't alone in this one. Eventually he acted, falling on his knees before God. Here's what he said:

> *"O my God, I am ashamed and blush to lift up my face to You, my God: for our iniquities have increased over our head and our guilt has grown up to the heavens. Since the days of our fathers we have been in a great guilt to this day and for our iniquities we, our kings, our priests have been delivered into the hand of the kings of the lands, to the sword, to captivity, to plunder, and to confusion of face, as it is this day. And now for a brief moment favor has been shown from the* Lord *our God, to leave us a remnant to escape and to give us a nail in His Holy Place, so our God could lighten our eyes, and give us a little reviving in our bondage . . . And now, O our God, what will we say after this? For we have forsaken Your commandments . . ."*
> (Ezra 9:6–8,10)

He feared dreadful consequences, the history of their people spoke loud and clear on this. Others did too and he was soon joined by *a very great congregation of men and women and children, for the people wept very bitterly* (Ezra 10:1). Among them was Shechaniah, who confessed his guilt on taking a foreign wife and suggested they make a new covenant with God to cast out their pagan wives. Ezra acted on this initiative and declared that all the Jewish men should assemble within three days for a mass confession and act of repentance. It rained throughout, which seemed quite fitting. But most came and perhaps, by their actions, they could have forestalled another ejection from the land.

How easy it had been for the Jews, even when back in their promised land, to fall back into the old ways and neglect the God Who had led them out of exile. How quickly they forgot God's great deeds on their behalf. How quickly they neglected Him, choosing to forget the penalties for doing so, punishments endured again and again by their forefathers.

"Neither will you make marriages with them! You will not give your daughter to his son, nor will you take his daughter for your son. For they will turn away your son from following Me so they may serve other gods, so the anger of the LORD will be kindled against you and destroy you suddenly."
(Deuteronomy 7:3–4)

Yet, once reminded, they were quick to act.

"And Ezra the priest stood up and said to them, you have been unfaithful and have taken foreign wives to increase the guilt of Israel. Now therefore make confession to the LORD, the God of your fathers, and do His pleasure and separate yourselves from the peoples of the land and from the foreign wives. Then the whole congregation answered and said with a loud voice, as you have said, so must we do."
(Ezra 10:10–12)

Applications for us today should not just be confined to our choice of marriage partner, but to anything that takes us away from God. Where are the Ezras today to remind us how far *we* have strayed away from what should be God-centred lives?

The Book of Nehemiah

The central message of this book is what to do if God puts a vision in your heart and how you must see it through, despite any opposition you may face.

Nehemiah had heard that, many years after the initial work done by Zerubbabel, the walls of Jerusalem were crumbling and the gates burned. He was greatly moved and prayed passionately that God would act on this, but decided to *take the initiative*. This is interesting, as the biblical norm seems to have God taking the initiative and tasking someone with a divine mission. Not in this case! As cup-bearer to King Artaxerxes (the probable son of Queen Esther, who had, a few years earlier, sent Ezra to Jerusalem), he had unprecedented access to him and asked him this:

> *"And I said to the king, if it pleases the king and if your servant has found favor in your sight, that you would send me to Judah, to the city of my fathers' sepulchers, so I can build it."*
> (Nehemiah 2:5)

He was sent off with the King's blessing. But not all were happy. Opposition was expressed initially in the hearts of two men, Sanballat and Tobiah. The first was a *Samaritan* (mixed-race, probably with Moabite blood) official of the Persian empire. The other was an *Ammonite*.

In Jerusalem, Nehemiah approached the people of the city:

> *"Then I said to them, you see the distress that we are in, how Jerusalem lies waste and its gates are burned with fire. Come, and let us build up*

the wall of Jerusalem, so we are no longer a reproach. Then I told them of the hand of my God which was good upon me, as also the king's words that he had spoken to me. And they said, Let us rise! Let us build! So they strengthened their hands for this good work."
(Nehemiah 2:17–18)

So the work commenced. Sanballat and Tobiah, now joined by Geshem the Arabian, were not happy and started their campaign of opposition. Nehemiah rebuked them: *The God of Heaven will Himself give us success. Therefore we His servants will arise and build, but you have no portion, or right, or memorial in Jerusalem* (Nehemiah 2:20).

The campaign against Nehemiah was stepped up and Sanballat now recruited his brothers and the Samaritan army into his opposition faction. Nehemiah was full of righteous anger and prayed:

*"Hear, O our God, for we are despised, and turn their reproach upon their own head and give them for a prey in a land of captivity. **Do not cover their iniquities ! Do not let their sin be erased from before You!** For they have provoked You to anger before the builders."*
(Nehemiah 3:36–37 – this is Nehemiah 4:4–5 in other versions)

More escalation, and now the Arabs and Ashdodites joined the opposition faction and words gave way to actions. The builders needed to take self-defence measures, working with one hand, a weapon in the other. When the wall was virtually finished, a sinister plot was hatched. The three protagonists suggested that Nehemiah meet them in a village. Nehemiah was wise to this:

"But they thought to destroy me. And I sent messengers to them saying, I am doing a great work, so that I cannot come down. Why should the work cease, while I leave it and come down to you?"
(Nehemiah 6:2–3)

They tried this tactic four times then, finally, Sanballat sent his servant with a letter, falsely claiming that Nehemiah's true intention was to become a King of the Jews. He ignored this but was troubled when he heard of a plot to assassinate him. But, when the walls were finally finished we read that the adversaries finally threw in the towel:

"And it was that when all our enemies heard and all the nations that were around us saw these things, they were very downcast in their own eyes, for they perceived that this work was wrought by our God."
(Nehemiah 6:16)

It was still an era of tribal gods, where each nation had their own *governing* god to call on. From back to the days of Moses, these nations always knew in their heart of hearts, that there was *something special* about this God of Israel. It didn't stop them from opposing Him, though, as we've seen. That very act had often been a *hardening* bestowed on them by God Himself, for His purposes. As we've seen with Nebuchadnezzar and the Persian kings, the God of Israel was acknowledged as the only true God. But still, the drama had to play itself out.

So Nehemiah stuck at his task, which was finally completed. It's what happened next that puts the reasons for such opposition into context.

"And all the people gathered themselves together as one man in the street that was in front of the Water Gate and they spoke to Ezra the scribe to bring the book of the Torah (Teaching) of Moses, which the LORD *had commanded to Israel. And Ezra the priest brought the Torah (Teaching) before the congregation, both men and women, and all who could hear with understanding on the first day of the seventh month. And he read there before the open place that was before the Water Gate from the daylight until midday, before the men and the women and those who could understand, and the ears of all the people were attentive to the book of the Torah (Teaching)."*
(Nehemiah 8:1–3)

The people wept and it was declared, *this day is holy to the* LORD *your God*. A few days later they celebrated the feast of Succot (Tabernacles), *the first time since the days of Joshua* and Ezra read from the Torah every day to the people.

Now we start to see the reasons for so much opposition to the rebuilding of Jerusalem from the Ammonites, Moabites, Samaritans and Arabs. It follows on from the reforms originally initiated by Ezra.

> *"And the seed of Israel separated themselves from all foreigners and stood and confessed their sins, and the iniquities of their fathers."*
> (Nehemiah 9:2)

They had to realise that they needed to purify themselves from the alien and pagan influences, a lot that had come through intermarriage. All things that, you'll remember, God had warned them about centuries earlier at the time of Moses and Joshua, necessitating what, today, we emotively call *ethnic cleansing*. There was now an amazing rededication back to God.

> *"And the rest of the people, the priests, the Levites, the gatekeepers, the singers, the Nethinim, and all those who had separated themselves from the peoples of the lands for the Torah (Teaching) of God, their wives, their sons and their daughters, everyone having knowledge and having understanding: they clove to their brothers, their nobles and entered a curse and an oath to walk in God's Torah (Teaching), which was given by Moses the servant of God, and to observe and do all the command-ments of the* LORD *our God and His judgments and His statutes. And that we would not give our daughters to the peoples of the land or take their daughters for our sons."*
> (Nehemiah 10:29–31 – this is Nehemiah 10:28–30 in other versions)

What is amazing about this whole story is that it was initiated by one man, Nehemiah, a layman, not a religious leader. He was not driven by a direct command from God but by the promptings of his own conscience, undergirded by God's teachings that were surely part of the DNA of righteous Jews of his day. Even Ezra, although a priest and a scribe, was driven by his duty as a Torah scholar to bring his people back to their God, rather than by an epiphany or divine intervention.

What a picture for us! The future of the Church is not solely dependent on the "professional Christians", the *clergy*, by whatever various titles they may be known. All faithful believers have their part to play.

Nehemiah was just like you and me, really. He needed his reassurances. *Remember me, O my God*, he cried. *Do not ignore my good deeds that I have done. Spare me according to the greatness of Your loving kindness* (Nehemiah 13:22). And then, finally, *remember me, O my God, for good* (Nehemiah 13:31).

Sometimes we just need to do what we know is right in God's eyes, rather than waiting for God's hands to nudge us into action. Nehemiah's actions were practical and Ezra's were more spiritual, but both equally had the result of drawing Israel back to their God. For that reason you can rest assured that God considered them *good and faithful servants*.

Surely we are in a desperate need for some Nehemiahs and Ezras in our generation.

The Book of Malachi

Here was the final biblical prophet of the Hebrew Scriptures. He lived in Jerusalem with the exiles who had returned and whom he observed continually slipping back into the *bad old ways*, despite all the sterling work of Ezra.

"A son honors his father and a servant his master. If then I AM Father, where is My honor?! And if I AM Master, where is My respect?! Says the LORD of Hosts to you, O priests who despise My name. And you say, how have we despised Your name? You offer polluted bread upon My altar,

then you say, How have we polluted You? In that you say, the table of
the LORD is contemptible."
(Malachi 1:6–7)

What on earth was going on here? God was being seriously
disrespected and by the *priests* of all people! When we remember
what the penalties were for *strange fire* in the times of Moses,
you can imagine how close these wicked priests were to their
own personal destruction!

". . . I have no pleasure in you, says the LORD of Hosts, neither will I
accept an offering at your hand."
(Malachi 1:10)

God then gives them a glimpse of the true scope of His plan
for the ages. A God *whose Name will be great among the nations*
is being treated here with less regard than their own governors.
They were literally bringing down curses on themselves.

"Behold, I shall corrupt your seed and spread dung upon your faces, even
the dung of your solemn feasts and one will take you away with it. And
you will know that I have sent this commandment to you."
(Malachi 2:3–4)

He couldn't have made Himself clearer. Malachi continues
in their condemnation:

"But you have departed from the Way, you have caused many to stumble
at the Torah [Teaching], you have corrupted the covenant of Levi, says
the LORD of Hosts."
(Malachi 2:8)

The Way is the way the people of God should walk according
to His commandments. These priests weren't just neglecting
their duties, but they were deflecting God's people from their

destiny, as a witness to the world of how a "chosen people" should be. And, to cap it all, they failed to understand why their offerings were being rejected.

> *"So this you do again: you cover the altar of the LORD with tears, with weeping, and sighing because He will not turn to the offering any more, nor to accept your good will offering."*
> (Malachi 2:13)

And because these pesky priests were starting to get on His nerves, the focus then shifts to future times, to an event where He was going to be *far more proactive* in the affairs of mankind.

> *"Behold, I am sending My messenger and he will prepare the way before Me, and the LORD Whom you seek will suddenly come to His Temple, even the messenger of the covenant, in Whom you delight. Behold, He will come, says the LORD of Hosts."*
> (Malachi 3:1)

John the Baptist, then the Messiah himself! It is worth now skipping to the final utterances of God's final prophet, until John the Baptist finally appears on the scene:

> *"Remember the Torah (Teaching) of Moses My servant, which I commanded him in Horeb for all Israel, even statutes and judgments. Behold, I AM sending to you Elijah the prophet before the coming of the great and dreadful Day of the LORD, and he will turn the heart of the fathers to the children and the heart of the children to their fathers, lest I come and strike the earth with a curse."*
> (Malachi 3:22–24 – this is Malachi 4:4–6 in other versions)

What does this tell us about what is important for us? The Torah of Moses, for a start. Then the return of Elijah the prophet, a role to be initially fulfilled by John the Baptist but surely, in the context of the Day of the LORD (which is still to come) ultimately fulfilled by *Elijah himself.*

The very last verse is quite intriguing:

"And he will turn the heart of the fathers to the children and the heart of the children to their fathers, lest I come and strike the earth with a curse."

Surely this hasn't happened yet, as Elijah hasn't yet returned. But when he does come, us dads and our kids *are going to have to get our act together.* But, seriously, surely this speaks about the centrality of family structures in God's plans. Yet in our modern society, *fatherhood* is under the greatest attack and is the most neglected and trivialised relationship dynamic of all. There's a big job out there for today's Church, if it is willing to get its hands dirty.

In fact, it's just one of *many jobs* that the Church needs to take seriously. Yet many in the Church are hamstrung because of their neglect of the Hebrew Scriptures, the *Old Testament.* Hopefully, now that we have completed our sweep of these Books, you can see how there is much we can learn from them, as well as the unique insight they give us to the Ways of God Himself.

So what have been the main points? It's time to draw strands together . . .

PART TWO
Themes

**Drawing together the strands
and making observations,
some of them quite surprising**

Some things we learn about God

There's a lot that the Hebrew Scriptures tell us about God. You would be surprised if they didn't, as every book that we read tells the reader something about the writer. In fact, this very book you're reading should tell you that *this particular writer* is as concerned with the bye-ways as the highways, as he believes that there are shed-loads of books out there concerned with the latter. So that's his excuse for any omissions in this chapter. This is not meant to be an exhaustive study, just a series of observations that may have passed you by but should prick your imaginations and pique your interest. So here we go . . .

God does all He can to grab our attention

We are perfectly capable of reading God's Word and missing His Voice. It may be that we're in a hurry to "read today's portion", because we're behind schedule or have a load of other stuff to do afterwards. Or perhaps we just don't have our spiritual antennae tuned, either through a crisis of faith, a general despondency or through a perceived over-familiarity with the text.

This is why a simple yet welcoming feature of the *One New Man Bible* is the use of **bold text** to indicate when God is *really* trying to grab our attention and is basically shouting at us! And there's an *awful lot* of bold text there. It also sets God up as a real Personality, a rounded Individual who occasionally needs to stress something important. That tells me that God really does want us to engage with Him through His word. So, in the Creation story, He shouts things into existence; light, the firmament, the waters, the land, the living creatures. **Be fruitful!** He cries. Then, His next piece of shouting is to Abram, comfortable in his father's house in Haran. **Get yourself out of here!** He shouted, as would a concerned modern Father to a child who has bedded in for the day in front of the TV set!

He also tells Moses to shout at Pharaoh, **Send My People away**! Later on He urges Joshua to obey the Torah and, in all things **Do not tremble! Do not be dismayed!** This, or the gist of it, is repeated to Joshua all through his career. He just needed to keep on obeying, even when the tasks he was asked to do, were not totally to his liking. When Samuel visited Jesse, God made it clear to Him that His choice of King had nothing to do with external appearances. **Do not look at the height of his stature** . . . He implored Samuel, before encouraging him to ignore the beefy brothers and select the more visually appealing David!

God uses the most unexpected people to carry out His plans

He chooses whom He chooses. That was true of the Nation of Israel, that small, noisy, contrary and stiff-necked people. And it was also true of those individuals whom He selected to carry out His plans. Now there's a case for declaring that just about every character that God chose from His own people was *flawed*. Abraham may have been the father of faith, but he showed little of this when sojourning with Sarah in Egypt. Moses may have been depicted by the manly and charismatic Charlton Heston in the movie, but wasn't he the reluctant leader who said *I am slow of speech and have a slow tongue*? You'd be hard pressed to find a King of Judah or Israel without some major character fault; Saul was impetuous and unforgiving, Solomon had a weakness for (lots of) unsuitable ladies, even David had his cunning and selfish moments.

But, for a God of Covenant, who places great store in what
He is planning to achieve through His Covenant people – the
Hebrew Nation and then Judah and Israel – He is not averse
to using people, even nations, from *outside* this Covenant, to
achieve His purposes.

He used the Egyptian Pharaoh at the time of the patriarchs,
to allow the life of Joseph to play out and to provide physical
salvation to the Children of Israel. You can even see the reverse
of this particular coin in that the later nastier Pharaoh was used
as part of the story of Moses and the Exodus, in order to forge
the Children of Israel into a nation, united by a single cause of
returning to their promised land.

He used Ruth the Moabite, a picture of selfless devotion to
her Jewish mother-in-law and her identification with the *people
of the Covenant*. She was so honoured that she was a part of the
exalted line that led to Jesus and was, in fact, King David's great
grandmother. But then, many generations later, He was to use
Nebuchadnezzar, the Babylonian King, as the instrument to
ensure exile for His faithless people of Judah and also, through
his troubling dreams, as a means for Daniel to rise to promin-
ence in Babylonian society and be a part of God's purposes
accordingly. Then there was a succession of Persian Kings,
Darius, Cyrus and Artaxerxes, all of whom were prompted by
God, and often acknowledging this fact, to ensure that the Jews
were to return to their land and rebuild their Temple.

The constant theme in the Hebrew Scriptures is of God using
Nations *outside* His covenant in order to bless or punish His
covenant Nation. In most cases the Nation that He used to
chastise the Hebrews are not just unaware of the *invisible strings*
controlling their actions but are puffed up in their own apparent
strength and openly hostile to the God of the Hebrews. This
always comes back to haunt them.

The evil Pharaoh may have had his heart hardened by God,
but there was enough free-will in the mix to ensure that he
wasn't a total patsy. And it was all for God's purposes, *so that*

future generations should know that "I AM the LORD". We also read of Nations that Joshua needed to defeat in order to claim the Promised Land: *For it was of the LORD to harden their hearts, so they would come against Israel in battle, so he could utterly destroy them* (Joshua 11:20).

When he was laying siege to Jerusalem, the Assyrian King boasted that every other god had crumbled before him and the God of Judah would be no different. So the God of Judah destroyed most of his army in one night and the King was later murdered by his own sons. Nebuchadnezzar, after boasting of his greatness and erecting a statue of himself for all to worship, ends up tethered and eating grass until he acknowledges who was the True God!

The Hebrew Scriptures are full of warnings and judgements against those Nations that came against His people, despite the ultimate Divine purpose. You can read these in Joshua, 1 & 2 Kings, Isaiah, Zephaniah, Nahum, Obadiah, Habakkuk, Ezekiel, Daniel and Nehemiah and lots of other places too.

God really *is* in charge and He will continue to use others in your life (as well as you in theirs) to fulfil His purposes in the long term. Our task is to discern when this is happening and not to resist it.

God does things in His own way and to His own schedule

We read earlier that Cain's big mistake could well have been a matter of timing, he simply didn't act *when* he was supposed to act. God decided to create the universe and everything in six days. He *could* have done so in microseconds (as the Church Fathers tended to believe) or billions of years (as evolutionists believe), but He told us, in His Word, that it took six days. If something doesn't seem logical, or fair, or reasonable to us, we tend to reject it. This is a big mistake, but is unfortunately a result of 2,000 years of *Aristotelian* thinking in the Church (for more of this read my book, *How the Church Lost the Truth*).

Jonah felt that God was unreasonable to want to save the evil city of Nineveh. So he ran away and became a fish dinner. Yet even in this act of defiance, God was able to use him to reveal Himself to his shipmates and save their souls. The people of Judah in Babylonian exile felt that it wasn't time to repair the Temple back home, but Haggai reminded them otherwise:

"Thus says the Lord of Hosts saying, this people says, the time has not come, the time that the Lord's House should be built."
(Haggai 1:2)

So God raised up three individuals, Darius the King, Haggai the prophet and Zerubbabel the governor and His Will was done, in His own timing. Soon after that, He did the same with Cyrus and Artaxerxes along with Ezra and Nehemiah. It was always a matter of timing, God's timing, perfect timing. He also provided a prophecy to Daniel that would provide a timeline for the coming of the Messiah, Jesus. It wasn't to happen for hundreds of years, but the timing was all laid out there for all to see.

All Job knew was that things were bad for him and getting worse. Yet his immediate reaction was that God knew what He was doing. Of course *we* rarely leave it at that and, as we saw with Job's discussions with his friends, we look for meanings and reasons behind everything. Yet the truth was in fact encapsulated in that very first reaction, *The Lord gave and the Lord has taken away. Blessed be the name of the Lord.*

God reminds us in His summing up to Job, that he has no credentials whatever to query the One who created the world, the land, the sea, the stars and all life on earth. He repeats this later through Amos.

"He Who made the seven stars, Pleiades and Orion, turns the shadow of death into the morning, makes the day dark with night, Who calls for the waters of the sea, and pours them out over the face of the earth,

the LORD is His name, Who causes destruction to break out on the strong,
so that destruction will come against the fortress."
(Amos 5:8–9)

God prefers it if we don't mess Him around

If prizes could be given out for moaning, the Children of Israel in the desert would have hit the jackpot. Despite the miracles of deliverance they witnessed, they still didn't always have sufficient trust that God would supply their physical needs. *"Lord"*, cried Moses, *"for how much longer am I to carry these people?"* Anyway they demand meat (despite their behaviour falling to a new low), so He gave them meat, lots of it . . . followed by a plague. Later on, the spies sent out to survey the Land of Milk and Honey, who gave a false report . . . were wiped out by plague, too. Even later on, at Baal Peor, the people *began to commit harlotry with the daughters of Moab.* The result? Another plague – this one wiped out 24,000 people!

When Joshua had destroyed Jericho, Achan stole an *accursed thing* and brought immediate judgement on the assembly and the death of his family. You simply *do not mess* with God! Then there were the sons of Eli the priest, who stole food meant for sacrificing and cavorted with women outside the Tabernacle. They met an untimely death, as did their father. Even errant kings, such as Saul, had to learn the lesson.

". . . Because you have rejected the word of the LORD, He has also rejected you from being king."
(1 Samuel 15:23)

Uzzah may have seemed an unfortunate recipient of God's wrath, when he touched the Ark, but he should have known better.

"And the anger of the LORD was kindled against Uzzah, and God struck him there for his error. And there he died by the Ark of God."
(2 Samuel 6:7)

King David, God's special favourite, also wasn't exempt. The penalty for adultery and the lies and deceit that surrounded it, was the death of his child. Then the inadvisable census he took resulted in the death of 70,000 men. King Solomon, as a result of his dalliances with pagan women and their gods, died in middle age, a confused and bitter man. But, if you think these early Kings were bad, they were not a patch on the later ones, particularly the Kings of Israel.

These are all strong lessons for us and are good reasons why we need to be well acquainted with these potted biographies in the Hebrew Scriptures. We may not be Jews, or Kings or prophets, but we are the same kind of fallible human being as they were. If we don't heed the lessons of their misdemeanours, then perhaps we are a people with no excuse.

God often does more than He is given credit for

In the sense that history is His Story, we often neglect the fact that the Bible may speak of the exploits and failings of human beings, but it is still . . . *His Story*. It's not always obvious. For example, the Book of Esther does not mention God once. But when you look at Esther and Mordechai's actions and motivations, you realise that this is where God is very much present. Similarly with Nehemiah. An ordinary person, who didn't see wonderful visions or hear divine voices; who was driven by the promptings of his own conscience, undergirded by God's teachings. Even Ezra the priest and scribe, was driven by his duty as a Torah scholar to bring his people back to their God, rather than by an epiphany or divine intervention. Again, Ecclesiastes fails to mention the LORD once by His name because it was written by a man, King Solomon in later life, who had lost his intimacy with his Creator and any mention of God was in the third person. God has allowed us to read this and learn from it. So, even when God is not explicitly mentioned, we can still learn many things, even if it concerns His absence in a man's life.

Perhaps the biggest lesson often missed by the leaders and Kings of Judah and Israel was that their successes were not due to *their* own efforts, only their failures were! Did they really believe that a generation of slaves could defeat the battle-hardened Amalekites through some sort of innate military canniness?

> *"And it happened, when Moses held up his hand, that Israel prevailed:*
> *and when he let down his hand, Amalek prevailed."*
> (Exodus 17:11)

No, this wasn't because Moses was controlling a belt-fed machine gun. He was simply following God's instructions, however strange they may have seemed at the time. God had a habit of doing that. Witness the highly complex sacrificial system, with its exact measurements and detailed instructions that had to be carried out to the letter! It may just be that, by doing so, God was asking them to take Him more seriously and not for granted. Sometimes He requires us to partner with Him in these joint endeavours. It's all very well expecting Him to win the battles for us or accept our sacrifices, but there always has to be *something* we have to do, even if it is just praying (not that this is an insignificant activity!).

Now the Children of Israel knew of this principle as early as their nervous wait at the edge of the Sea, when Moses declared: **"Do not be in awe!** *Stand still! See the salvation of the* LORD, *which He will show you today, for the Egyptians whom you have seen today, you will see them again no more forever. The* LORD *will fight for you, and you will hold your peace"* (Exodus 14:13–14).

When Achan stole *the accursed thing,* God temporarily removed His protection over Joshua's army and they were defeated in battle, losing 36 men. When Achan's sin was discovered and dealt with, they resumed the battle and this time slaughtered 12,000 of their enemy.

For the battle is not yours, but God's. This is still true for us today.

God reveals more about Himself than we usually notice

God has poured Himself into the ink on your printed Bible. Until we individually learn to hear His voice in other ways, the printed Word is all we have. It's a shame that it is a second hand Word, translated from a language that is both beautiful and impenetrable, into that of our everyday speech. What we gain from having the words in English, we lose through missing the nuances and subtleties of Hebrew. That is, unless the translator is tuned into the Hebraic mindset and can pick these up. The *One New Man Bible* is a step in a right direction, but nothing can substitute for the *real thing*.

God reveals Himself in the first case by the very Name that He uses for Himself at any given time. As Creator He is *Elohim*, the main word that is translated as God, but as soon as He gets personal with His Creation, He begins to use His personal name, *YHWH*, the word that appears as LORD in our English Bible. The word is considered too holy to leave in its original Hebrew, so the Jewish scribes substituted it with the word *Adonai*, Hebrew for Lord, but printed as LORD in this divine context. YHWH was not meant to be pronounced but, as a *reminder* that it must be read as *Adonai*, the vowels for this latter word are assigned to YHWH, simply as a memory aid. Unfortunately, Gentile Christian translators had been ignorant of this fact and attempted to pronounce this word, as *Jehovah*, a word that is meaningless to the God to Whom it is meant to refer! Others have chosen to attempt to vocalise YHWH as *Yahweh*, but this writer tends to believe that if God has wanted us to pronounce His name then He would have supplied us with the vowels Himself.

As we progress through Scripture we see a variety of Names He uses for Himself, from the generic title *El*, to the variations of *Eloah* (used in Job) and *Elah* (an Aramaic variation) as well as compound words such as *El Shaddai* and *the Lord of Hosts*, all appearing for particular reasons at certain times.

And this leads us to a very important principle. As a chief function of Holy Scripture is to draw people back to their Creator, it is paramount that He is properly represented. We need an authentic vision of God, so that we can appreciate Him properly. Many, if not most, of His actions are to that end and He has a neat phrase for it; *for My Name's sake*. We have already seen this in Ezekiel:

> *"Therefore say to the House of Israel, Thus says Adonai, the* Lord, *I* AM *not doing this for your sake, O House of Israel, but for My holy name's sake, which you have profaned among the nations wherever you went. And I shall sanctify My great name, which was profaned among the nations, which you have profaned in their midst, and the nations will know that I* AM *the* Lord, *says Adonai, the* Lord, *when I am sanctified in you before their eyes."*
> (Ezekiel 36:22–23)

He needs a good Name, a good reputation, so you can see that when Israel had profaned His Name, this was not good and results in dire consequences. Yet He persevered with His people and promised them (in the next few verses in Ezekiel) that He *still* had a great future planned for them. God does *not* go back on his promises. He repeats this in 1 Samuel 12:22 and reminds His people that He is only holding back His wrath *for His Name's sake*, because it is wrath they surely deserved (Isaiah 48:9).

Both Jeremiah (Jeremiah 14:7,21) and the Psalmists understood this and remind God of His great attributes, His forgiveness (Psalm 25:11), guidance (Psalm 31:4) and salvation (Psalm 79:9) and they are all good demonstrations of His good Name.

Surely it should make us tremble in an age when even some Christians are surely *profaning His Holy Name* in their actions. Is He forestalling judgement *for His Name sake* or is the Church ripe for a major shock?

Finally we can't finish speaking of our God without a reference or two about *His amazing grace*. Some Christians

consider the "Old Testament" a place where grace is in short
supply and where an angry God indulges in smite-fests and
unreasonable demands on His people. How wrong is that!
Without His *amazing grace* surely He would have given up on
us in the Garden of Eden, let alone the incredible patience
shown to the long chain of flawed people that He uses for His
purposes? But, if you want specific examples . . .

King Ahab, husband of the evil Jezebel, was an absolute
disaster, of whom it was said, *there was no one like Ahab, who sold
himself to work wickedness in the sight of the LORD.* Yet, we also
read that he later went through a change and repented of his
actions. And what did God do? *Do you see how Ahab humbles
himself before Me? Because he humbles himself before Me, I shall not
bring the evil in his days, but I shall bring the evil upon his house in
his son's days* (1 Kings 21:28–29). That is *amazing grace*. We also
saw it in the story of Jonah, when, to Jonah's disgust, God
decides that Nineveh, the capital of the evil Assyrian Empire,
was to be given a chance to mend its ways.

And what about that megalomaniac, Nebuchadnezzar? He
saw the light and was reprieved by God.

> *"And at the end of the days I Nebuchadnezzar lifted up my eyes to heaven,
> and my understanding returned to me and I blessed the Most High and I
> praised and honored Him Who Lives Forever, Whose dominion is an
> everlasting dominion, and His kingdom is from generation to generation."*
> (Daniel 4:31 – this is Daniel 4:34 in other versions)

Amazing Grace. Sometimes it grates! Always it cleanses,
restores and heals.

Some things we learn about man

What we need to realise is that, when we read about the exploits (and failings) of the Hebrew people (from Abraham to Malachi) in the Hebrew Scriptures, they are not a peculiar species of mankind, but simply representatives of us all. There is no doubt that, by and large, if any of us were replanted into Bible times, we would make the same mistakes and suffer the same temptations as they did. So all of my conclusions here are generic ones, they apply to *all of us*.

Sometimes we don't know what is good for us

God laid it out very simply in His Word:

> *"I'll call heaven and earth to witness this day against you, I have set before you life and death, blessing and cursing. Therefore **choose life**, so both you and your descendants may live."*
> (Deuteronomy 30:19)

Surely it's a *no-brainer*. Trouble is, human beings can be brainless creatures in choices they make. Quite often it is because we are creatures of impulse, giving in to the moment regardless of the consequence. This needs to be overcome, because what God offered then – and still does – is a long-term relationship. This is laid out in the following verse:

*"So you can love the L*ORD *your God, so you can obey His voice and you can
cleave to Him, for He is your life and the length of your days, so you can stay
in the land which the L*ORD *swore to give to Abraham, to Isaac and to Jacob."*
(Deuteronomy 30:20)

Deuteronomy 28 spells out the formula very explicitly, so
much so that, looking back, we can see the whole of Jewish
history laid out. They had a choice, there's always a choice. But
they didn't always choose life.

King Solomon was reminded of this:

*"But if you will at all turn from following Me, you or your children, and
will not keep My commandments and My statutes which I have set before
you, but go and serve other gods and worship them, then I will cut off
Israel from the land which I have given them, and this House, which I
have sanctified for My name, I shall cast out of My sight and Israel will
be a proverb and a byword among all people."*
(1 Kings 9:6–7)

God spoke thus for a purpose. He knew that Solomon was
wavering and about to make many wrong choices, connected
to the number of pagan concubines he was to add to his harem.

God doesn't go back on His promises, but neither does He
fail to carry out a promised punishment. Solomon's subsequent
acts split the kingdom in two, then, a few years later, the acts
of his son's usurper, *Jeroboam*, were to ensure exile for the
Northern Kingdom. Later on the same happened to *Manasseh*,
the evil king of Judah, whose acts were to ensure exile for the
Southern Kingdom. Neither of these acts met fulfilment in the
lifetime of the chief culprit, but the curses were *never rescinded*,
even if subsequent Kings were better behaved. A good example
of this is King Josiah:

*"And there was no king before him like him, who turned to the L*ORD *with
all his heart, and with his entire being, and with all his might, according*

to all the Torah (Teaching) of Moses, nor did any like him rise after him. Nevertheless the LORD did not turn from the fierceness of His great wrath, by which His anger was kindled against Judah because of all the provocations with which Manasseh had provoked Him."
(2 Kings 23:25–26)

But there are blessings too. We read of the story of Zerubbabel, in the Book of Haggai. He obeyed God and took Him seriously, in starting the rebuilding of the Temple. As a result, Zerubbabel attains a place in the exalted Messianic line, leading to Jesus. What a legacy!

Some of us start well but finish very badly

There are some startling lapses and collapses with some characters in the Hebrew Scriptures. King Solomon has been mentioned, the man who went from this:

"And Solomon's wisdom excelled the wisdom of all the children of the east country, and all the wisdom of Egypt. For he was wiser than all men, even Aitan the Ezrahite and Haiman and Calkol and Darda, the sons of Mahol: and his fame was in all nations round about. And he spoke three thousand proverbs: and his songs were a thousand and five."
(1 Kings 5:10–12 – this is 1 Kings 4:30–32 in other versions)

To this (in a couple of decades):

"Better is a poor and a wise child than an old and foolish king, who will no longer be admonished."
(Ecclesiastes 4:13)

Another King who couldn't sustain his relationship with God was Asa, King of Judah. At the start of his reign, he both cleansed his kingdom of pagan religion and urged his people to follow the Torah. But he ended his reign as an oppressor of his people and eventually died of a foot disease that God would have healed, if he'd only asked!

How many of us know Christians who have been on fire for the Lord but who have allowed the flames to dwindle, even die out? Perhaps if Solomon and Asa had godly and trusted advisors (as David seemed to have in Nathan), they could have remained strong in the Lord?

Perhaps we need to ensure that we are accountable too, by surrounding ourselves with wise and godly men and women who are not afraid to question and correct our actions and motives? And for us to develop the humility to listen and act where necessary!

Some of us have forgotten the central message

The purpose of The Bible is not to feed our brains with the stories of God's struggles with His people, but rather to *inspire our heart* to learn from these struggles. It provides us with a way of life, depicted as "the Way of the Lord". The central message is therefore to do with our deeds, our acts rather than our knowledge and understanding. This is often missed, so it's worth perusing some Scriptures that speak of this:

> *"For I know him, that he will command his children and his household after him and they will keep the Way of the* Lord, *to do acts of loving kindness and judgment, so the* Lord *may bring upon Abraham that which He has spoken of him."*
> (Genesis 18:19)

> *"And you (Moses) will teach them ordinances and Torah (Teaching) and will show them the Way in which they must walk and the work that they must do."*
> (Exodus 18:20)

> *"They (the Israelites) have turned aside quickly out of the Way which I commanded them."*
> (Exodus 32:8)

*"**Behold!** I AM setting before you this day a blessing and a curse; a blessing, if you obey the commandments of the LORD your God, which I command you this day and a curse, if you will not obey the commandments of the LORD your God, but turn aside out of the Way which I command you this day, to go after other gods, which you have not known."*
(Deuteronomy 11:26–28)

"Nevertheless the LORD raised judges who delivered them out of the hand of those who plundered them. And yet they would not listen to their judges, but they went astray after other gods and bowed themselves to them. They turned quickly from the Way in which their fathers walked, obeying the commandments of the LORD, but they did not do so."
(Judges 2:16–17)

"For the LORD knows the Way of the righteous, but the way of the ungodly will perish."
(Psalm 1:6)

In fact the Psalms (as well as the Proverbs) are full of references to *The Way*, which shouldn't surprise us.

But if we want a verse that really explains what *The Way* actually is, it is this one:

*"He has shown you, O man, what is good. **And what does the LORD require of you, but to do justice, to love loving kindness, and to walk humbly with your God?!**"*
(Micah 6:8)

It's all about obeying God and doing what He asks, living sacrificial lives full of good works to others. By doing so we are actually worshipping God. The God of the Bible could well be more pleased with the person in the Church kitchen joyfully preparing refreshments, than the one in the Church hall singing, but with his heart disengaged. Here's a verse that speaks into this:

"And Samuel said, has the LORD as great delight in burnt offerings and sacrifices as in obeying the voice of the LORD? Behold, to obey is better than sacrifice, to listen is better than the fat of rams."
(1 Samuel 15:22)

It's better that we're doing things wholeheartedly rather than going through the motions, because God knows us only too well.

". . . For the LORD does not see as man sees, for man looks at the outward appearance, but the LORD looks at the heart."
(1 Samuel 16:7)

There was even a point when God was thoroughly fed up with "religious" sacrifice and spoke through Amos:

"I hate, I despise your feast days and I shall not smell the burning sacrifices in your solemn assemblies. Though you offer Me burnt offerings and your meal offering, I shall not accept them. Nor will I even glance at the peace offerings of your fat beasts."
(Amos 5: 21–22)

When we read *burnt offerings* and the like, we must think of our modern equivalents, our worship songs, our rituals, even our good works, when they are done out of *anything other* than a willing heart. We need to be motivated by love, of man and God, and allow this to inform our actions.

Cleanliness really is close to godliness

Now, of course we know that this phrase is nowhere to be found in the Bible. Yet there's hardly a truer statement!

We start in Leviticus. Over a third of all mentions of cleanliness in the Bible are in this book. God wanted to ensure that they ate healthily, so He provided many food regulations. But there was another kind of cleanliness, a *spiritual* kind. The whole purpose of the offerings and sacrifices so meticulously

described in this book were *to make His people clean before Him.*
It was an inner cleanliness that He spoke of:

> **"Do not turn to idols, or make molten gods for yourselves!** I AM the
> LORD *your God!"*
> (Leviticus 19:4)

Idols, false gods, familiar spirits, wizards, witchcraft, they
are all *unclean.* They were filth to the soul. God's people were
warned again and again to distance themselves from these
abominations. It is interesting that, for the priests, inner cleanliness had to be accompanied by *outer cleanliness.*

> *"And the LORD spoke to Moses saying, "Take the Levites from among the
> children of Israel and cleanse them. And you will do thus to them to
> cleanse them: Sprinkle purifying water upon them and let them pass a
> razor over all their flesh and let them wash their clothes, and so make
> themselves clean."*
> (Numbers 8:5–6)

At the sacking of Jericho, Achan's sin that brought such
judgement was to pollute himself with *that accursed thing,*
which in turn made him *that accursed man* and sealed his fate.
God cannot abide spiritual uncleanliness. Hence the nature
of the destructions of the cities they came across. Everything
had to be destroyed, for God's *kingdom of priests* to remain
clean.

Remember how Isaiah described himself. *I am a man of
unclean lips and I live in the midst of a people of unclean lips, for my
eyes have seen the King, the LORD of Hosts* (Isaiah 6:5). He also
implored his people, *Make yourselves clean! Put away the anarchy
of your doings from before My eyes! Stop doing evil!* (Isaiah 1:16–17).

We Christians may be cleansed by the blood of our Saviour,
but God's people in the Hebrew Scriptures had no such
provision, so they just had to do the best they could to stay pure

and undefiled. Unfortunately, as we read again and again, it was their leaders who let them down.

> *"For Solomon went after Ashtoret the goddess of the Sidonians, and after Milkom the abomination of the Ammonites. And Solomon did bad things in the sight of the LORD, and did not go fully after the LORD, as had David his father."*
> (1 Kings 11:5–6)

> *"Ahab made an Asherah and Ahab did more to provoke the LORD God of Israel to anger than all the kings of Israel who were before him."*
> (1 Kings 16:33)

This is why the prophets were needed.

> *"I AM knows Ephraim, and Israel is not hidden from Me. For now, O Ephraim, you commit harlotry, Israel is defiled. They will not frame their doings to turn to their God, for the spirit of harlotry is in their midst and they have not known the LORD. And the pride of Israel testifies to His face, therefore Israel and Ephraim will fall in their iniquity, Judah also will fall with them. They will go with their flocks and with their herds to seek the LORD, but they will not find Him. He has withdrawn Himself from them."*
> (Hosea 5:3–6)

Their uncleanliness brought the ultimate judgement, exile from their land.

CHAPTER

Some other things we learn

Of course there's loads we can learn and a whole library of books is needed to convey the whole story. But what we have focused on are three key ongoing stories that provide a necessary bridge not just to the New Testament, but to our lives today and in the future.

Jesus really is splashed all over the place

Firstly, the bridge to the New Testament. How was Jesus foretold in the Hebrew Scriptures? Well, where *wasn't* he foretold? There's probably a case for digging up a Messianic prophecy in virtually every book of the Hebrew Scriptures, but here are the ones already highlighted in this book. We have looked at the Psalms and then showed Messianic expectations in the words of seven of the prophetic books.

The Psalms cover some of his life, a lot on his death and still more on his future reign on Earth. Here's an example of the latter:

> "... So the nations and all the kings of the earth will revere the name of the LORD Your glory. When the LORD will build up Zion, He will appear in His glory. He will regard the prayer of the destitute and not despise their prayer. This will be written for the generation to come, and the people that will be created will praise the LORD."
> (Psalm 102:16–19)

Hosea speaks of Jesus' sojourn in Egypt (Hosea 11:1), Isaiah speaks of the virgin birth (Isaiah 7:14), the Messianic titles (Isaiah 9:5–6), the character of Jesus as suffering servant (Isaiah 53) and the Messianic "calling card" (Isaiah 61:1–2). Micah identifies Bethlehem as Jesus' birthplace (Micah 5:1), Jeremiah speaks of the New Covenant (Jeremiah 31:30–33), Daniel predicts a date when the Messiah is to come (Daniel 9:25–26), Zechariah gives a number of prophecies about the first and the second coming (Zechariah 6:12–13, 11:12–13, 13:7, 9:9–10 and 14:9) and Malachi predicts John the Baptist (Malachi 3:1).

It really is undeniable when we see them all together, but many will still deny who he was and why he came. This is a battle we have been called to fight, in an age where secularism is currently winning the war for hearts and minds.

The Jews have an undeniable future

This is the bridge to our lives today and the fact that Jews are a part of our lives today should be all the proof we need of God's unconditional and everlasting covenant with them. Yet some seek to deny this.

The main ports of call are the prophets. It is said that every prophetic book speaks on this theme, but we will list just four of them here:

"And it will be in that Day, the Lord will set His hand again the second time to recover the remnant of His people, which will be left from Assyria, from Egypt, from Patros, from Cush, from Elam, from Shinar, from Hamath, and from the islands of the sea. And He will set up a sign for the nations, and will assemble the outcasts of Israel and gather together the dispersed of Judah from the four corners of the earth."
(Isaiah 11:11–12)

*"In that Day it will be said to Jerusalem, **Do not fear!** To Zion, **Do not let your hands be slack!** The LORD your God is mighty in your midst! He will deliver! He will rejoice enthusiastically over you with joy! He will rest in*

His love, He will rejoice over you with singing. I shall gather those who are sorrowful for the solemn assembly, who departed from you, to whom the reproach of it was a burden. Behold, at that time I shall undo all that afflicts you and I will save her who halts and gather her who was driven out, and I will get them praise and fame in every land where they have been put to shame. At that time I shall bring you back, even in the time that I gather you. For I shall make you a name and a praise among all the peoples of the earth, when I turn back your captivity before your eyes, says the LORD.*"*
(Zephaniah 3:16–20)

"Therefore, behold, the days are coming, says the LORD, *that they will no longer say, the* LORD *lives, Who brought the children of Israel from the land of Egypt, but the* LORD *lives Who brought up and led the seed of the House of Israel out of the north country and from all the countries where I had driven them when they will live in their own land."*
(Jeremiah 23:7–8)

"For I shall take you from among the nations and gather you out of all the countries and will bring you into your own land. Then I shall sprinkle clean water upon you and you will be clean from all your filthiness and from all your idols. I shall cleanse you. And I will give you a new heart and I will put a new Spirit within you and I will take away the stony heart from your flesh and I will give you a heart of flesh. And I shall put My Spirit within you and cause you to walk in My statutes and you will keep and do My judgments. And you will dwell in the land that I gave to your fathers and you will be My people and I AM *will be your God".*
(Ezekiel 36:24–28)

With regards to this prophecy, it is worth repeating what was said earlier. *For His holy Name's sake*, God is going to return Israel to their land, in order to eventually turn them back to Him. So, if we miss this, *then we are missing a self-declared act of God*, for His holy Name's sake.

Those Christians who miss this fact, either through ignorance or prejudice, who can't admit that the birth of modern Israel is not just history but *His Story*, then they are **denying the One they claim to serve**. This is serious.

There's a lot that hasn't yet happened

Finally, this is the bridge to our lives in the future. It has been said that a significant number of prophecies in the Hebrew Scriptures haven't yet been fulfilled. We now place ourselves into the highly contentious area of End Times, including the return of Jesus Christ and the Millennial Kingdom. When Christians disagree about anything, rather than exploring argument and counter-argument it's good just to read the Scriptures for yourself and let them sink into your spirit:

> *"And He will judge among the nations and will decide among many peoples. And they will beat their swords into plowshares and their spears into pruning hooks. Nation will not lift up sword against nation, neither will they learn war any more."*
> (Isaiah 2:4)

> *"But He will judge the poor with righteousness and decide with equity for the humble of the earth and He will strike the earth with the rod of His mouth, and with the breath of His lips He will slay the wicked."*
> (Isaiah 11:4)

> *"The wolf also will dwell with the lamb and the leopard will lie down with the kid, and the calf and the young lion and the fatling together, and a small youth will lead them."*
> (Isaiah 11:6)

> *"Then the eyes of the blind will be opened, and the ears of the deaf will be unstopped. Then the lame man will leap like a deer and the tongue of the mute will sing, for waters will break out in the wilderness and streams in the desert."*
> (Isaiah 35:5–6)

*"In that Day it will be said to Jerusalem, **Do not fear!** To Zion, **Do not let your hands be slack!** The Lord your God is mighty in your midst! He will deliver! He will rejoice enthusiastically over you with joy! He will rest in His love, He will rejoice over you with singing. I shall gather those who are sorrowful for the solemn assembly, who departed from you, to whom the reproach of it was a burden. Behold, at that time I shall undo all that afflicts you and I will save her who halts and gather her who was driven out, and I will get them praise and fame in every land where they have been put to shame. At that time I shall bring you back, even in the time that I gather you. For I shall make you a name and a praise among all the peoples of the earth, when I turn back your captivity before your eyes, says the Lord."*
(Zephaniah 3:16–20)

"Thus says the Lord, I have returned to Zion and will dwell in the midst of Jerusalem and Jerusalem will be called The City of Truth and the mountain of the Lord of Hosts, The Holy Mountain."
(Zechariah 8:3)

"Behold, I am will make Jerusalem a cup of trembling for all the peoples round about, when they and Judah will be in the siege against Jerusalem. And in that Day I shall make Jerusalem a burdensome stone for all the peoples. All who burden themselves with it will be severely injured, though all the peoples of the earth are gathered together against it."
(Zechariah 12:2–3)

"And it will be in that Day, I shall seek to destroy all the nations that come against Jerusalem."
(Zechariah 12:9)

Read these again and ask yourself, *have any of these prophecies actually happened yet?* If the answer is negative, then, secure in the knowledge that God doesn't lie and that He also doesn't seek to confuse or deceive us, then all of this is yet to come.

And the only ones who should worry about this are those who are not in God's Kingdom, but should also include those who are in the Kingdom, but *not yet totally* aligned with it.

Epilogue

The journey ends, but it also begins because you should now be so excited about God's Word that you are going to read it afresh. The Hebrew Scriptures may have these thirty nine divisions, each with their unique style and emphasis, but it is important that we sense the unity that connects them, the narrative of the Holy Spirit, guiding us into all truth.

I think that if there is one truth that for me encapsulates the central message of the Hebrew Scriptures, it is this: **God prefers a people who sincerely obey Him to a people who insincerely worship Him**.

Now is this heresy I preach, because we are surely created to worship Him and surely, when all is wrapped up, we will join the Heavenly Host in Revelation 4:8:

> *"And the four living creatures, each one of them having six wings, all around and within they were full of eyes, and they do not have rest day and night saying, "Holy, holy, holy, Lord God of Hosts, Who was and Who is and Who is coming."*

Yet – and this is a personal opinion – surely He is more pleased with those cheerfully making the tea in the small kitchen than with some in the sanctuary who are stretching out their hands and bellowing worship songs, *but are mostly thinking about that nice cup of tea waiting for them at the break*. If I am honest, there have been many times when "worship time" has conflicted with my state of mind. I am *not always* ready to sing songs, or smile and act like I'm connecting with God. Perhaps we should develop a Church culture where some of us can sometimes opt out from compulsory "praise & worship" and, instead, help with the tea making, or whatever task needs doing?

> "And Samuel said, has the LORD as great delight in burnt offerings and sacrifices as in obeying the voice of the LORD? Behold, to obey is better than sacrifice, to listen is better than the fat of rams."
> (1 Samuel 15:22)

The building up of a people who follow *The Way* is surely the point of both the Hebrew Scriptures (Old Testament) and the Greek Scriptures (New Testament)?

> "He has shown you, O man, what is good. **And what does the LORD require of you, but to do justice, to love loving kindness, and to walk humbly with your God?!**"
> (Micah 6:8)

> "Every way of a man is right in his own eyes, but the LORD ponders the hearts. To do acts of loving kindness and justice is more acceptable to the LORD than sacrifice."
> (Proverbs 21:2–3)

Never in Scripture do I see God castigating people for performing righteous deeds, but I do see many Scriptures where God states how tired He is of ritual and tired worship, where the act itself is not driven by a sincere heart. And I'm not just talking about 'Strange Fire'.

So the key is our sincerity before the Lord. When we worship Him, whether through song or acts, it should be sincere and wholehearted. When we perform our deeds, let them be righteous, in accordance with His words and direction and also done wholeheartedly, in love and not reluctantly or unthinkingly.

And that's all I'm going to say on the subject, it is now up to us to ask Him how we can put these words into practice.

Finally, one thing we need to cement to our soul is the one priceless and often misunderstood fact that all Scripture declares, and it is this:

All that God does in the affairs of mankind is for His Glory, His Name's sake, in order to draw people to Him, in order that they may live eternally with Him.

> *"Therefore say to the House of Israel, Thus says Adonai, the* LORD, *I* AM *not doing this for your sake, O House of Israel, but for My holy name's sake, which you have profaned among the nations wherever you went. And I shall sanctify My great name, which was profaned among the nations, which you have profaned in their midst, and the nations will know that I* AM *the* LORD, *says Adonai, the* LORD, *when I am sanctified in you before their eyes."*
> (Ezekiel 36:22–23)

This general principle is not just acted out in the pages of the Hebrew Scriptures, but also in the New Testament, when we see that the primary objectives of healings and miracles is not for our well-being but as a witness to lead people to salvation. In the same way, all that we do should be for His Glory, so that by our actions, we are drawing people closer to the Kingdom.

In conclusion, this journey has been a wonderful God-led experience for me. It has been a joy, a privilege and an education to write this book. I can only pray that it has been the same for you and all that's left for us is to reach for our Bibles and to get back into God's Word.

I do believe He has a few things yet to show us and teach us, but all in keeping with His nature so wonderfully revealed in *God's Blueprint*.

Now why don't you . . . ?

At the current time nine of my books are still available for purchase, either through Amazon, Christian bookshops or directly from www.sppublishing.com.

To Life! – *Rediscovering biblical Church*

Have you ever asked the question, where does the World end and the Church begin? Is the 21st Century Church truly the best it could possibly be?

> "In this fine book, Steve Maltz addresses the issue of religious tradition and its power to force out biblical truth, thus creating disarmed and impotent churches. It is a warning we must heed."
> (**Chris Hill**, Bible teacher, writer, broadcaster)

How the Church lost The Way . . . –. . . *and how it can find it again*

The story of how the Church has been infiltrated by a pagan virus that has worked its way through every facet of our Christian life and how we can start fighting back.

> "With great insight, explaining many concepts simply, Steve Maltz brings us back to the root of our Christian faith. I believe that every pastor and ordinand in the country will benefit from reading this book."
> (**Mark Weeden**, Senior Pastor, Worthing Tabernacle)

How the Church lost The Truth . . . – . . . *and how it can find it again*

What has happened to some key battlegrounds of Christian Truth and how it is that the Church has managed to lose so much that had been revealed to it in the Bible.

> "I really enjoyed reading it. You are the master of epigrams, full of Jewish wit and humour, which I love. These keep you reading and make the whole interesting. It's so important to add gravy to the meat and you are a good chef. I hope this book will reach those who need it most though I fear they will be irritated, if not infuriated, by your dismissal of so many of their heroes!"
> (**David Pawson**, international Bible teacher)

Jesus, the Man of Many Names – *A Fresh Understanding from the dawn of time to the End of Days*

Are you prepared for a new book about Jesus that does offer fresh insights without boasting new revelations? Drawing on sources from the Jewish world, ancient and modern, the author will take you on an exhilarating, lively and entertaining exploration of the life and times of the Jewish Messiah.

"Steve Maltz has a gift for combining pacy writing with crystal-clear distillation of his own careful study of scholarly resources and a firm grip on the Gospel. The result is a fascinating new landscape of insight"
(**David Andrew**, editor *Sword Magazine*)

The Truth is out there – *The Ultimate World Conspiracy. Who really is pulling the strings?*

Is history just a random sequence of events, or are there secret manipulations? What makes us tick? How did the World as we see it come to be? Read this book if you are prepared to be challenged.

"Steve Maltz has a rare gift of being able to communicate complex ideas in a way that leaves you thinking that you have read the work of a genius but can still follow his argument clearly. A brilliant read for an evangelist to engage with a sceptic or to give as a gift for 'food for thought'."
(**Tim Leffler**, The GoodBookstall.org.uk)

The (other) F-Word – *Faith, the Last Taboo*

A presentation of the Gospel for the modern world. It is direct, uncompromising, engaging and is written to be relevant to the everyday person. Dare you go where modern man fears to tread? You'll either be inspired or provoked, either way it should be an interesting experience.

"This is a clear and straightforward evangelistic book, written with real style and panache, and a genuine sense of humour. But at the same time it is serious and God-honouring. I genuinely think that not since C. S. Lewis have we had a Christian author who has addressed his current generation in such a culture-attuned way."
(**Peter Sammons**, author and publisher)

Outcast Nation – *Israel, The Jews . . . and You*

The story of the People and the Land through biblical and secular history, tracing the outworkings of God's covenants and offering explanations for both the survival and the success of this Outcast Nation.

> *"The 'Unavoidable Questions' in the final chapter are particularly challenging, and need to be answered honestly, however uncomfortable they may make you. Highly recommended for reading by as many people as possible, of all beliefs and none."*
> (**Mary Bartholemew**, The GoodBookStall)

God's Signature – *The Wonders of the Hebrew Scriptures*

Have you ever wondered how the Old Testament came to be written, why God chose Hebrew as the language of the Book and what exactly could we be missing through not reading the Hebrew Scriptures in their original language?

> *"For those who want a readable introduction to the matter or for those who simply want to dip their toes into the subject God's Signature is definitely the book to start with. You'll find it very difficult to put down."*
> (**Mike Moore**, Director of Christian Witness to Israel)

The Bishop's New Clothes – *Has the Church Sold out to the World?*

Is the Church as it should be or has it sold out to the World? Is the Body of Christ doing all it could as God's ambassadors or is there room for not so much an improvement as a complete overhaul? This book pulls no punches, but it does so engagingly, with wit and warmth. **If you think all is well in the Church in the west, be prepared for a major shock.**

"The One New Man Bible *aims to bring greater understanding of and appreciation for the power given to believers for their daily walk. In the words of the Preface:* 'The One New Man Bible . . . makes the Jewish roots of Christianity come to life' *having been* 'edited from a public domain English translation. The English has been brought up to date and many words previously translated according to tradition have been changed to the literal. The New Testament is the Power New Testament, a fresh translation of the Fourth Edition United Bible Society Greek Text. An effort has been made to keep the text as free as possible from denominational biases and doctrinal interpretations . . .' My verdict? This book is more than a useful addition to the serious Bible student. It is something that every such student should have available. Would it be a reliable stand-alone, general purpose Bible? My first impression was 'no' but I have to say that with use this fresh translation does 'grow' on me as a reader. I am enjoying it more and more. I believe that over the next 20 years this fresh translation will become far more widely adopted. It is priced competitively with higher quality translations."*
(**Peter Sammons**, writer and publisher)